GREAT MINDS

Your World...Your Future...YOUR WORDS

- Inspirations From South & South East England

Edited by Steve Twelvetree

 Young**Writers**

First published in Great Britain in 2005 by:
Young Writers
Remus House
Coltsfoot Drive
Peterborough
PE2 9JX
Telephone: 01733 890066
Website: www.youngwriters.co.uk

SB ISBN 1 84602 193 6

Foreword

This year, the Young Writers' 'Great Minds' competition proudly presents a showcase of the best poetic talent selected from over 40,000 up-and-coming writers nationwide.

Young Writers was established in 1991 to promote the reading and writing of poetry within schools and to the youth of today. Our books nurture and inspire confidence in the ability of young writers and provide a snapshot of poems written in schools and at home by budding poets of the future.

The thought, effort, imagination and hard work put into each poem impressed us all and the task of selecting poems was a difficult but nevertheless enjoyable experience.

We hope you are as pleased as we are with the final selection and that you and your family continue to be entertained with *Great Minds - Inspirations From South & South East England* for many years to come.

Contents

Aylesford Secondary School, Aylesford

Bennett Memorial Diocesan School, Tunbridge Wells

Grace Simpson (12)	62
Jordan Tomkins (12)	62
Elliott Bailey (12)	63
Sofia Protopsaltis (13)	63
Alex Wathen (12)	64
Yasmin Dunnett (11)	65
Natalie Grew (12)	66
Hannah Washbrook (12)	67
Matt Cole (12)	68
Sally Megan Maric (12)	69
Elysia Pike (12)	70
Emma Christopher (11)	71
Lloyd Mitchener (11)	72
Cheryl Moss (13)	73
Hannah Price (12)	74
Amy Shepherd (12)	75
Ellie Thomas (11)	76
James Palmer (12)	76
Katie Neal (11)	77
Zoe Slater (13)	77
Hannah Luxton (11)	78
Sophie Bright (12)	79
Jake Elder (11)	80
Lauren Hooper (11)	81
Stephanie Bartlett (12)	82
Lauren Troke (12)	83
Beth Clarke (12)	84
Jack Ingram (13)	84
Frances Procter (12)	85
Victoria Frampton (11)	85
Vicky West (12)	86
Jessica Howe (13)	87
Joshua Horn (13)	88
Adam Mitchell (12)	88
Jennifer Singleton (12)	89
Robert Ineson (12)	89
Ania Gould (11)	90
Andrew Salmon (11)	91
Helen Duyvesteyn (12)	92
Hannah Roberts (12)	93
Charlotte Ivey (12)	94
Dan Pugh (12)	95

Natasha Underwood (11) 96
Elisabeth Dean (12) 97
Katherine Brown (13) 98
Adam Refoy (12) 99
Brett Champion (12) 100
Ben Miles (13) 101
Emma Cran (13) 102

Chatham Grammar School for Girls, Chatham

Frances Sales (11) 102
Bethany Eves (12) 103
Sarah Mace (12) 103
Yasmin Gayle (12) 104
Helen Coote (12) 104
Rebecca Payne (13) 105
Amy McElwaine (11) 105
Kimberly Hoather (11) 106
Sophie Byrne (11) 106
Stephanie Powell (11) 107
Connie Rogers (13) 107
Naomi Bathgate (13) 108
Marie Hart (13) 108
Stephanie Broodbank (12) 109
Alex Cachia (12) 109
Jessica Pocock (13) 110
Lucy Essenhigh (13) 110
Victoria Gibbs (12) 111
Toni Paterson (12) 111
Hannah Starr (13) 112
Rebecca Birch (13) 113
Stephanie Cornwell (12) 114
Nicola Dobinson (12) 114
Rosemary Brennan (12) 115
Victoria Walton (12) 115
Paige Gibson (13) 116
Stephanie Coney (12) 116
Sarah Andrew (12) 117
Amy Le Conte (12) 117
Megan Davis (11) 118
Adekunbi Okufi (13) 119
Sarah Burley (13) 120

Cranford House School, Wallingford

Rebecca Apley (13)	149
Hayley Jubb (12) & Michelle Sangan (13)	150
Emma Griffin (13) & Katie Allen (12)	150
Lucy Goodyear (12)	151
Zenia Selby (10)	151
Courtenay Argyle (13)	152
Georgina Lindsey (12)	152
Katherine Poulter (13)	153
Jessica Leslie (14) & Katherine Sandbach (12)	153
Charley Grimshaw (11)	154
Gemma Bridge & Rosie Jackson (11)	154
Annabel West & Jenny Robinson (11)	155
Olivia Beazley (11)	155
Eleanor Chappell (12)	156
Amy Sansom (11)	156
Lauren Field (12)	157
Esther Irving (11)	157
Poppy Jackson (11)	158
Rebekah Donald (12)	159
Rosie Miller (11)	160
Paige Lingwood (12)	160
Katrina Allen (13)	161
Gracie Miller (11)	161
Fiona Hildred (12)	162
Emily Sansom (11)	163
Carly Goggin (12)	163
Genevieve Moody (12)	163

Danley Middle School, Sheerness

Anna Berrisford (11)	164
Angharad Lanning (11)	164
Jason Binfield (11)	165
Thomas Cantellow (11)	166
Jade Charles (11)	167
Katelin Thomas (11)	168
Faye Saunders (11)	169

Dunottar School, Reigate

Jessica Dawson (12)	169
Verity Lambert (14)	170
Megan Clarke (12)	171
Beatrice Kerslake (12)	172
Emma Telford (12)	172
Ashling Ramdin (11)	173
Charlotte Hutchinson (11)	173
Victoria Godefroy (12)	174
Zoe Case-Green (12)	175
Nadia Harper (11)	175
Carolyn Bullimore (11)	176
Joanna Childs (11)	177
Sarah Clement (12)	178
Madeleine Stansfeld (12)	179
Sophie Flanagan (12)	179

Enfield County School, Enfield

Rosean Fernando (14)	180

JFS School, Kenton

Adam Rutstein (15)	180
Claudia Cramer (15)	181

King Ethelbert School, Birchington

Taylor Ann Davies (11)	182
Kirsty Reed (13)	182
Christian Meah (11)	183
Hannah Alexandrou (12)	183
Owen Connolly (14)	184
John Dean (12)	184
Alyce Cronk (12)	185
Nicola Baldwin (12)	185
Danielle Neat (12)	186
Samantha Bale (12)	186
Jamie Saunders (13)	187
Tanya Wilson (11)	187
Robert Edwards (12)	188
Alison Hutchinson (11)	189
Rachael Hammond (13)	190

Melissa Coupland (11)   219
Jessica Osbourn (12)   220
Gemma White (14)   221
Andrew Denton (14)   222
Hayley Pemble (13)   223
Andrew Lucas (12)   224
Gemma Peverett (12)   225
Amy Heath (12)   226
Lois Hetterley (14)   227
Matthew Ayling (14)   227
Sinead Hallett (14)   228
Joshua Mincher (14)   229
Jade Dugggan (11)   230
Tamara Joyce (13)   231

Longford Community School, Feltham
Marina Qattan (11)   231
Emma O'Brien (11)   232
Hayley Elliott (12)   232
Carly Parker (12)   233
Emily Gates (12)   233
Lana Louise Watters (11)   234
Lewis Metcalfe (12)   234
Bryan Dollery (15)   235
Jade Stroudley (12)   235
Rhys William Last (12)   236
Adam Fowler (12)   236
Samantha Baldwin (15)   237
Billie Stephana Brockway (12)   237
Wendy-Hannah May (14)   238
Jack Johnson (12)   238
Bhavina Vadgama (12)   239
Jessica Bellfield (12)   239
Chantel Faye Dyte (11)   240
Kathryn Evans (11)   240
Rachel Twohey (15)   241
Charles Byrne (11)   242
Lauren Woods (11)   242
Amelia Mullen (12)   243
Georgie Giddings (14)   243
Laura Cripps (15)   244

Wallington High School for Girls, Wallington

Walmer School, Walmer

Whitton Secondary School, Whitton

The Poems

The Hawks Of Hell

White skies, inverted, can turn amazing black
Keyholes to what lies behind
Hell springs, as soon as you turn your back
Twisting your state of mind

No mercy, not even a scorching red, no devil's horns or tail
Just cobwebs, dull, boring black
Is the real definition of Hell

The skies are the hawks that hunt you down
Not the underground, that's where you're safe
With God and Jesus, if that's what you like
But in Hell, there is no belief

They don't judge you by what you do
They judge you by what you think
So keep your conscience clear
Or be jotted down
In irremovable ink.

Louisa Mokadem (11)

Great Minds

G ood imagination always helps
R ight thoughts pop in and out
E xcellent work gets you good grades
A friend who helps make it easier every day
T imed work is slightly harder.

M oney doesn't buy you the job you want
 I gnorance won't get you anywhere
N o one cares unless you're there
D one all the hard work that you can
S o it's up to you what you do right now.

Aliysa Louise Virani (12)

Untitled

It can't be found in silver
It can't be found in gold
Your love is inside you
Just let it unfold

If there is someone special
And you know deep in your heart
That you know love so much
You can't stand to be apart

Then take it with both hands
And make sure they know
Just in advance
That you will never let them go

Show them life
As hard as it may seem
Let them know they are loved
Make every moment like a dream

Rise above perfect
Be better than the rest
Show them the real you
And time will do the rest.

Caroline Songhurst (15)

Stronger

Feeling pressure
Feeling alone
No one understanding
No one at home
Feeling nothing
Only hate
Feeling sad
Scared of my fate
Can't be positive
Can't be glad
Feeling negative
Feeling bad

Feeling bored of being mad
Feeling happy, feel no sad
Seeing happiness
I'm not that bad
Feeling stronger
Getting braver
Feeling safe
Found my Saviour
Don't need help
Don't feel bored
Not afraid
Found the Lord

Not helpless
Happy for longer
Looking happy
I'm much stronger!

Emily Whitmarsh (13)
All Saints Catholic School, West Wickham

The Young Maiden

Through the field, where the flowers grow
Up to the gate, where the wind does blow
There sits a young maiden
With grief, she is laden
For her declared beau will not show

She let him go, some years ago
Whether he was dead she did not know
To war he went, and left the young maiden
To weep in 'sweet old meadow'

Then came old news, about her beau
For he was killed, by neither friend or foe
She started to sorrow, and felt all craven
Just like how Eve must've felt in the Garden of Eden
For her grief, she let the tears flow
In 'sweet old meadow'.

Natalya Mykhaylyuk (12)
Alperton Community School, Wembley

Friends

Friends are like family,
They grow together
Being as strong as rock, as soft as sponge
We look out for each other
As lions look for zebras
Our friendship is not racist
As we take in different races
Whether you're African or Indian
It makes you equal
Even if you are the only one wearing braces
So if you think about it
It makes your friendship extra special.

Liam Graham (12)
Alperton Community School, Wembley

Up A Mango Tree

When I'm up a mango tree
I see the world before me
I see the view for miles around
It simply couldn't bore me!

When I'm up a mango tree
The sun's rays shine upon me . . .
Peace and tranquillity soothes and surrounds
Stress just simply ignores me!

When I'm up a mango tree
The animals don't disturb me
Hummingbirds, caterpillars, bumblebees
They all absolutely adore me!

When I'm up a mango tree
The world is at peace with me
I love my big old mango tree
And my mango tree loves me!

Alia Coleman (13)
Alperton Community School, Wembley

In The Wild

I move in a mysterious way
I have wonders to perform
I plant my footsteps quietly
As I stride along
I treasure the long grass that I hide behind
Creeping in the shadows of my prey

When the time comes I leap out
I don't mean to take another life
It's the only way to survive . . . a cheetah's life!

Sandeep Patel (12)
Alperton Community School, Wembley

She Stood There With A Whip In Her Hand

She stood there with a whip in her hand
Dominating the classroom
Her eyes were fixed on me, I knew it
I was treading on the path of doom

She stood there with a whip in her hand
Staring continuously at me
The volcano would soon erupt
Why did it have to be me?

She stood there with a whip in her hand
I really needed to cough
I was definitely in it for now
I jerked a little. There was no hope now

She stood there with a whip in her hand
Her prying eyes had seen me
She moved to her feet and walked up to my desk
She would definitely destroy me

She stood there with a whip in her hand
She opened her mouth
'You're in for it now,' she screamed
I should have just migrated south

She stood there with a whip in her hand
The cracking of the whip I could hear
She lifted the whip above my head
And it cracked down on my ear

She stood there with a whip in her hand
All eyes were on me
My ear was red and it was burning
I stared at her in shame

She stood there with a whip in her hand
I stared at her in pain
I sat there embarrassed
Did it really have to be me?

Hetal Hirani (13)
Alperton Community School, Wembley

The Power Of Nature

Nature, nature
You're so great.
Nature, nature
Are you the reason life exists?
Nature, nature
Is it because of you there are four seasons?
Nature, nature
Are you the cause of day and night?
Nature, nature
Why are you so unfair?
Nature, nature
You don't seem to care.

Nature, nature
What was the point in causing the tsunami?
Nature, nature
Do you even know how many lives it took?
Nature, nature
Do you know this affected the whole world?
Nature, nature
You're the reason for the earthquake underwater.
Nature, nature
Why is there a dark side to you?

Nature, nature
Why is Earth the only planet that supports life?
Nature, nature
Why don't you stop for a moment and think
Then you'll see all the errors in you.
Nature, nature
Stop playing your silly games
Open your eyes and see how sometimes you can be a shame,
After all, nature
You will always be the one controlling everything.

Sobethan Nanthakumar (13)
Alperton Community School, Wembley

My Last Birthday

It's my birthday and I'm thirteen
The party's going well and we're watching Mr Bean
Everyone's singing and my candles are about
Everyone goes silent, *bang* and a gunshot is out
Lying on the ground with images of Mum
I just feel really, really numb
Down at the hospital, everyone is crying
They're saying I'll be fine, but I know that they're just lying
Everyone looks at me to show that they care
Death is a thought that I really can't bear
Everyone has to die sometime and my time is now
So bye-bye everyone, as I take my last bow.

Nevine Amer (13)
Alperton Community School, Wembley

Frightened

I see a shadow in the dark
And then I hear a dog bark
What was that? I say in my mind
I tried to search but couldn't find
Then I thought that I had seen
Something big and green
Could it be a monster?
No, it's a shadow of a lobster
Maybe this is all a dream
I open my eyes, see a light beam
The door opens, I see my mum
Oh, how could I have been so dumb?
My mum tells me, 'Don't fear,
Nothing will scare you my dear'
My mum told me right
I slept peacefully all night.

Nirali Suriacant (13)
Alperton Community School, Wembley

Friends Forever

Friends are special
Friends are true
If they're a good friend
They'll be there for you

We're all sad every once in a while
But if we have friends it ends in a smile
A dependable friend will never let you down
A dependable friend will never make you frown

But yet there comes a day
When friends may fall apart
But it doesn't last long
If your friend has a big heart

I have a friend
Who's kind and clever
And I know for sure
We'll be friends forever!

Moshgan Ahmadi (12)
Alperton Community School, Wembley

The Terrible Tsunami

26th December
A day to remember
A million lives it took
It'll be in the big history book
The Earth it shook
Visit those countries, just take a look
People dead, orphaned and homeless
It's left them foodless, aidless and waterless
Money they need
Let's collect the most and take the lead
They'll rebuild their lives slowly
While we just live coolly
'Help!' they shout
Don't you dare have a doubt!

Hiba Mohamad (13)
Alperton Community School, Wembley

I'm Sorry Friend

You were always there for me
Throughout the years
Whenever I needed you
You were always there for me

When I was lost, it was you that showed me the way
When I was sad, it was you that put a smile on my face
When I was in trouble, it was you that saved me

We shared everything, you and I
We laughed together
And cried together
It was me and you against the world!

But when you needed me, I turned and walked away
When you needed me, I neglected you and left you there all alone

I said to you things that I wish I hadn't
I hurt you friend
I made your heart bleed
I made the tears fall from your eyes

And for that, I'm sorry friend
I wish that I could take it all back
I wish that I could turn back the clock
And start all over again

I love you friend
You mean the world to me
And I hope that you can forgive me
Because I am really sorry friend.

Nikita Vyas (14)
Alperton Community School, Wembley

Friendship

Although it's quite a statement
It happens to be true
The best friend I've ever had
I'm glad to say it's you

You're there if I should need you
And you never turn away
I know that I count on you
Twenty four hours a day

We've had our problems
As nearly everybody does
But arguments never last that long
With special mates like us

Some people have so many mates
With whom they spend their time
But no one has a special mate
As fabulous as mine

So thank you for always being there
Your friendship's strong and true
And I just want to let you know
I'm always there for you

Through sun, rain, light, dark
On you I can depend
I always want to hear you say
Our friendship will never end!

Mohini Patel (13)
Alperton Community School, Wembley

Someone Special

I know someone special who's so nice
Who's very intelligent and very wise
I know someone on whom I can rely
Who will never break a promise
And then deny

She's so kind, loving, caring and understanding
With everyone and not just towards me
That if you spend a day with her
Then you will definitely see!

There is never a dull moment when she is around
Because her happy spirit turns you upside down
I admire her in each and every way
I wish I could be like her one day

She would always be ready to help
Whatever her circumstances may be
If I'm going through a bad phase
I know she will always be there for me

She's one in a million
A star in the sky
She's the best a friend could be
And I'm never going to let her pass by.

Bhavna Grover (14)
Alperton Community School, Wembley

Childhood Memories

I remember
I remember
The day of my first birthday!
My house was very crowded
It was 5 months after May

I was new at walking
So, I fell down every few steps
The guests were on foot and talking
My mother and father wept

The time had come
To cut the cake
The lights went down
A wish to make

The wish I took
Was very wise
I had to look
Deep inside

I wished for joy
I wished for no war
I wished for toys
But most of all
I wished for
Peace.

Sapna Samji (13)
Alperton Community School, Wembley

Him

I do not know his name
I do not care
But he lives in my neighbourhood
And I wish he was not there

His scrawny body
His coal-blackened face
His dusty, dirty hands
He looks a disgrace

His bad attitude
His evil grin
He is armed with a weapon
An empty, broken bottle of gin

Such an unpleasant human being
I wish he was gone
I wish he never existed
I wish he was never born.

Reuel Roberts (14)
Alperton Community School, Wembley

Racism

Why judge a person for the colour of their skin?
It's like throwing coloured paper in the bin
So what if you're black, white, brown or whatever
It's not going to change you from being clever

Black or white
Stop the fight
We all have made decisions
Of what religions
We would obey
So please, I pray
Bring peace, oh world!

Kiren Rao-Nebab (13)
Alperton Community School, Wembley

I'm The One

I am big, I am bad
I think that you're all freaks
So give it to me now
You're pathetic and weak!
What I have is what you need
The friends, the name, the look and the greed
I dominate the school
Because I have the power
My group and I, we rule them all
I stand over you like a tower
I will kick you and smash you
Abuse and harass you
Your clothes are rubbish!
Your hair is yuck!
You use words like chap
And you really stink
One day soon
Your defeat will come
You are doomed
You're just pond scum!

Nikita Shah (12)
Alperton Community School, Wembley

Being The Victim

I am being bullied
I don't like it a bit
If I was playing a game
I would always be *it*
I am hurt from being hit
They think I am thick
I cry each night and dread each day
It feels like I hate school
But I really don't
I wish I wasn't bullied.

Dharshika Pathmanathan (11)
Alperton Community School, Wembley

You Were Always There

Whenever I needed someone to talk to
You were always there.
My eyes filled with tears, my heart filled with pain and
You were always there.
There was no time when I had doubt
To come to you because
You were always there.
I could see in your eyes you wanted to help
And that you really cared.

Whenever I was down and blue
You were always there.
No matter my problems, or what was wrong
You were always there.
Whenever I felt like nothing matters
You were always there.

Now you're gone, and I don't know what to do
I close my eyes and think of you, and how
You were always there.
It's hard to look at the pictures, and get memories of you
Can you hear me now?
At night I pray and I speak to you
I guess you were right when you told me no matter how far you were
You would always be there.
I know one day I'll see you again, but till then I have to say goodbye.

Even though it hurts to hear your name and speak of you
One thing I will always say is
You were always there.

Abu Hanif (13)
Alperton Community School, Wembley

The Bully

I'm ferocious
I'm dangerous
I'm curious
And furious

Monday I stole
Tuesday they suffer in pain
Wednesday is a day of shame
Thursday is payback day
Friday I make them bleed
Saturday is when I rest in peace
Sunday I wait for Monday to start again

The cycle repeats
So we meet
I cover the victims in slime
But they never committed a crime

I'm strong, bold and caring
Who am I kidding?
You know me
I'm the bully

So innocently tempered
Who blames them?
I frequently blame others
Don't spare any
Even if they are in pairs
Staggering and climbing the stairs
I catch them unawares.

Kunal Patel (11)
Alperton Community School, Wembley

Power Rangers

I was about five when I used to watch
Power Rangers every day live
I used to love this back in the day
My mum and dad used to say,
'Turn the TV off and go play!
Haven't you got anything better to do on this day?'
But I watched my all action superheroes together
Chilling on my comfortable sofa's leather

I watched the Power Rangers for several years
Listening to the loud music and action in my ears
I loved it so much, I even bought the action toys
Everyone was going on about it, especially the boys

Everyone loved it because of the action
It was better than doing any type of maths fraction
The computer graphics caught everyone's attraction!

Several years later, when I was about ten
I was mostly at school writing with a pen
Every hour of every minute then got boring
During one programme my brother caught me snoring
Then I switched to another superhero called Spiderman
Now you'll find me his number 1 fan!

Rabiur Tarafder (13)
Alperton Community School, Wembley

Bullying

Bullying is so fun
Pushing people around
Fighting little boys
And being the king!
Watching the tears drip down the cheeks
What a beautiful scene it is
Short boys are the best
The ones on their own
Near the little corner!

Karan Datta (12)
Alperton Community School, Wembley

Memories!

Memories, memories you will never forget
The joyfulness, joviality, glee and blitheness
Will never abduct happy memories
The sweet sound of TV all day
And music showing the way

Memories, memories you will never forget
If I could recollect in my hood days
There was war all around me
War on poverty and drugs
Gangsters crazy over ballas
But that's how my life became
A misery from my earliest memory
That's just my prophecy!

Memories, memories you will never forget
They're like a huge maze
Some complimenting and some sorrowness
They all end up with one phrase
But I'm hopeful, yes I'm hopeful for today
I take these memories and let them take me away
I know it ain't easy but that's ok
Remembering memories end up in one way

Memories, memories you will never forget.

Yash Maniar (13)
Alperton Community School, Wembley

The Worst Life

They are fast, they are scary
They always pick on me day and night
They think I am a loser
They call me names
I wish they'd never been born
They are so evil that I think that God is never with me
They twisted my hand and I want revenge
I wish someone could help out
One boy came and asked, 'Why are you sad?'
I said, 'I am bullied and no one understands'
The next day was wonderful, the bullies never showed up
They had been expelled because of the little boy who helped me
'Hurray', I shouted, it was a wonderful day.

Maunika Selvarayan (12)
Alperton Community School, Wembley

Island Man

Morning
I wake up to the hotness of the skies
In my head
Ready for the beach

Mad seagulls
Ships out at sea
The sun shining bright

From the west
Of the tiny island
I will always come back

Come back to hot sand
Bright orange

Another Caribbean day.

James Harger (11)
Archbishop Tenisons CE High School, Croydon

Life As A Journey

My life has been uphill, downhill, uphill
I could have been dead
If it wasn't for my brother.
It all started when I was drowning
Down, down, deeper and deeper
Splash! The water rippled
It was my brother
He came to save me

I saw him, he reached out to me
He slammed me onto the side
He came to save me!

David Harger (11)
Archbishop Tenisons CE High School, Croydon

The Boy Who Saw A Pig Fly

There once was a boy who saw a pig fly
The boy said, 'Don't say goodbye,'
The pig stopped and turned his head
The boy thought he was dead

'Pig,' he cried
His mum thought he'd died
The pig rushed out
Without a doubt

The boy ran out to the farm
He ended up in the barn
Whoosh! The pig flew!
The boy slipped over like glue

The little boy started to cry
The boy said, 'Goodbye,'
The pig stopped and turned his head
The pig said, 'I'm going to bed!'

Rachel Jenner (11)
Aylesford Secondary School, Aylesford

The Sandman

Part One

It's late at night
The moon's in sight
And something's out to get him

The Sandman will rise
He's in for a surprise
And something's out to get him

The clock strikes eight
It's getting late
And something's out to get him

Off to bed
With a smack on the head
And something's out to get him

Dark stairs are long
Something's wrong
And something's out to get him

Run to the top
He's too scared to stop
And something's out to get him

Into his room and in his bed
Pulling the covers over his head
And something's out to get him

He can have the moon
He'll be here soon
And something's out to get him

He heard something creep
So he takes a peep
And something's out to get him

He's all alone
Cold as stone
And something's out to get him.

Samantha Ischt-Lipscombe & Maria Anderson (14)
Aylesford Secondary School, Aylesford

The Sandman

Part Two

The stairs start creaking
The boy starts freaking
And something's out to get him

It's opened the door
And is walking the floor
And something's out to get him

Into his room
To seal his doom
And something's out to get him

It's only his mum
He feels so dumb
And something's out to get him

From the shadows he appears
Bringing the boy's fears
And something's out to get him

He's jumping around
Not making a sound
And something's out to get him

Blowing the sand
From his hand
And something's out to get him

The Sandman tries
To steal your eyes
And something's out to get him

Flying into the night
The boy's lost his sight
And something's out to get him

The story is real
And how would you feel
If The Sandman was out to get you?

Lee Dunn (15)
Aylesford Secondary School, Aylesford

Lady Heather

Through the alchemist's potion
Lady Heather I spy
Has the look of an eagle
Through the blink of an eye

The growl of a tiger
Stuck in her throat
The anger she carries
Hides under her coat

Wishes for a man
Sworn never to hurt her
Unlike those before
Would he ever desert her?

Alone at a table
She sits and waits
An arrow her weapon
For Cupid's mistakes

Like a wolf she hunted
And bit at her prey
Now he is here
He is here to stay . . .

Maria Goodhew (14)
Aylesford Secondary School, Aylesford

Limerick

There was a young lady from Spain
Who was awfully sick on the train
She had the flu
And went to the loo
But never came back again!

Yasmin McCullough (12)
Aylesford Secondary School, Aylesford

Where Is He Now?

I woke up early before the sun
Thinking of my hero but now he has gone
Knock, knock . . .
On the doorstep did my hero stand before
Hope he's ok, fighting in the war

I ran downstairs
And stood still for
A minute, *knock knock . . .*
It went again, is it him, am I insane?

I opened the door; it was a tall dark man
Standing there with a letter bag
He handed me a letter and off he went
Would I ever see my hero again?

He's back there in those trenches
Serving us all with cold, smelly socks
Out on his own
Out in the snow, wind and rain
Will he come back?
Will I see him again?

Rosie Fry (15)
Aylesford Secondary School, Aylesford

Wintertime

W hite snow glistening in the lane
 I vy growing up the windowpane
N ight sky growing darker and darker
T oes defrosting by the nice warm fire
E mbers glowing shiny and bright
R elaxing, cosy in the dark of night.

Lara Sargeant (11)
Aylesford Secondary School, Aylesford

Battle

Bloody war
People die in front of me
People going over the top
Going no more

Ammunition has only one mission
That's to kill
Bullets and bombs
Only to kill

The trenches are muddy
You don't walk, you trudge through
Rats coming around
People lying dead

Terrified friends waiting to go over the top
Never knowing what's over there

Lovely, peaceful home
Children praying, never knowing
What it's like

Everybody I knew died
In that life on the battlefield.

James Davies (14)
Aylesford Secondary School, Aylesford

Football Match

The scream of the devoted parents
The smack of a player scoring a goal
The crying of an upset player losing
The crunch of an aggressive tackle
The stinging sound of the referee's whistle
The scorch of the ball hitting the net
The roar of the goalie shouting
All the noises you would hear at a football match.

Kenny Wilson (12)
Aylesford Secondary School, Aylesford

War

In the trenches here I stand
Keeping away from no-man's-land
Praying that my life be spared
I fear for my safety, I'm so scared
I feel empty and insecure
I stand lonely in this war

Beyond the wire awaits my fate
It's the men I'm told to hate
This sorrow feeling is all around
On this thought, I hear no sound
My heart stops pumping, I feel so drained
I don't want to be here, it's as if I'm chained

Here I am, forced to fight
I get through the day and struggle through the night
The sights I see increase my fear
Upon my cheek one single tear
The stench of death is all around
The cries of men, a deafening sound

Also I hear bullets flying
Watching the agony as men are dying
This whole war is full of madness
In my heart I'm filled with sadness
Awaiting the day I return home
It will be the day I'm no longer alone.

Josh Heskett (14)
Aylesford Secondary School, Aylesford

Recipe For A Perfect Football Match

Begin with 11 players
Add a teaspoon of Rooney's goals
And in the safe hands of Howard
Stir in lots of goals to beat the other team
Bake for 90 minutes
Serve with sweet victory.

Leroy Brown (11)
Aylesford Secondary School, Aylesford

Christmas

C andles glowing in the night
H eavenly stars shining bright
R osy cheeks by the fire glow
I vy-green against the pure white snow
S leepy children in their bed
T insel sparkling shiny red
M istletoe hung all around
A ll silent, not even a sound
S anta's coming, wait and see
          What a surprise for you and me!

Lola Inge (11)
Aylesford Secondary School, Aylesford

Newspapers

Why isn't it like they said?
Glory of the war
Tell that to him
The man over there with his leg shot off
They all say we are wanted and our country needs us
But all they want to do is lie - lie - lie
All those men gathered together
Such a waste of time
All that's gonna happen is they're gonna die - die - die.

Natasha Buss (15)
Aylesford Secondary School, Aylesford

The Woman Who Danced To Calais

There was a young woman from France
Who loved the can-can dance
She danced to Calais
In less than a day!
In a lively and jumpy prance!

Sophie Puddefoot (12)
Aylesford Secondary School, Aylesford

The Dead!

The bombs stop with a sudden echo
I walk into the dark, cramped trenches
Dead people sprawled everywhere
No one knows what's happened
There's a big blast, on a whistle
We all hear shouting
Then the rapid fire of machine guns
There is another blast of a whistle
It goes quiet, the bombs start again
I can tell we are going to be in that
Muddy, rat-infested trench for a long time.

Matthew Barnard (14)
Aylesford Secondary School, Aylesford

Cinema

The cinema doors bang open, as loads of people tumble in
Families are shown to their places
Seats are slammed down
The film starts, the lights turn off
People whispering and munching on their popcorn
Children shuffling and rustling empty wrappers
The film ends, the lights turn on
People clap and cheer.

Stacey Startup (12)
Aylesford Secondary School, Aylesford

Recipe For A Perfect Day

Begin with bags full of fun
Mix in some sport
A tablespoon of energy
A pound of excitement
Bake for 12 hours and
Serve with one happy 11-year-old.

Liam Lewis (12)
Aylesford Secondary School, Aylesford

Another Day Of The War

As I lay on the cold, hard floor of my trench
I look at the sky above and think about the day I just passed
The hundreds of lifeless soldiers that lay upon no-man's-land
The bitter wind amongst the air
The restless soldiers that trained and fought
It's just another day of the war

I'm absolutely exhausted, but I'm too scared to sleep
I feel isolated and glum
My hands and feet are numb
The food's unpleasant and nasty
The weather's frigid and raw
It's just another day of the war.

Joanne Fuery (14)
Aylesford Secondary School, Aylesford

The Cinema

The scramble of the people rushing in the door
The screaming of the kids grabbing their tickets
The clash of the till going in and out
The trampling of the people getting the best seats
The crunch of the food, the slurping of the drinks
The shuffling of the movements
The giggling of the girls in front
The loudness of the big screen all colourful and bright
The mumbling of everyone moving out their seats
The banging of the doors of everyone going
The echo of the last person that spoke
All quiet until more people come to
The cinema.

Gabrielle Frankham (12)
Aylesford Secondary School, Aylesford

Easter Eggs

Easter eggs are different shapes
Circular, oval and round
All sorts of different types
I watch them on the ground

Easter eggs in boxes
On the shopping shelf
I am going to buy two
All to myself

Easter eggs are lovely
Eaten all I can
I might have one more
I am the Easter eggs' biggest fan

Easter eggs in my tummy
I feel very sick
I don't want to see an Easter egg again
The chocolate eggs are so difficult to pick.

Lottie Jenner (11)
Bennett Memorial Diocesan School, Tunbridge Wells

Mud!

I run out onto the pitch
My first touch of the ball is magical
My first tackle is brilliant
I catch the ball and run, run, run

The ground comes rushing up at me
Boots, boots everywhere
Crashing down near me

I catch the ball and run, run, run
Nobody tackles me
I dive into the mud
And plant the ball

The try is mine!

Alistair Grice (12)
Bennett Memorial Diocesan School, Tunbridge Wells

He . . .

He sat silently in the sun's rays,
The breeze pushing upon him,
His dark hair free in the wind,
His feelings darkened with sin.

No one stirred from the grass around,
No noise was made nearby,
But the sea's waves and the cry
Of birds in the near-off sky.

He could smell the corpse around him,
With his head upon his knee,
The souls of those who fought here,
Now too far-off to see.

For war is not a great thing,
No heroes left behind,
Just those trying to search for,
That peaceful place to find.

Roanna Fawcett (13)
Bennett Memorial Diocesan School, Tunbridge Wells

Homeless

There I was, sitting by the roadside
It was so quiet it was as if I had died
All that was left were a couple of jars
People looked at me as if I was from Mars

I had my headscarf and my coat
I looked into my pocket and found a note
It was given to me when I was young
By my mum who had always sung

The song spun my head round and round
All I could hear was this beeping sound
The lorry sped past, I was too late
I will forever remember this date.

Ellie Heskett (11)
Bennett Memorial Diocesan School, Tunbridge Wells

Entertainment

Books, books I really like books!
Lord of the Rings or Harry Potter
Wind in the Willows or Barry Trotter
These are all names of really good books
So never judge a book by its cover or its looks!

Movies, movies I really like movies!
The Haunted Mansion or Die Another Day
Finding Nemo or The Month Of May
These are all names of really cool movies
So never say they're bad or you'll get the groovies!

Games, games, I really like games!
The Hungry Hippos or Monopoly
Guess Who or Chimpanzees
These are all names of really cool games
So never stop playing or you'll turn to flames!

Alicia Griffin (12)
Bennett Memorial Diocesan School, Tunbridge Wells

Swimming With Dolphins

Dolphins are beautiful
Streamlined creatures
They feel like silk and rubber
Unlike whales, they have no blubber
And enjoy playing around with each other!

I kissed him on the lips
I rode on his back
He did so many flips
I wish I could be with them all day long
Although the fish they had
Really started to pong!

Hannah Sainsbury (12)
Bennett Memorial Diocesan School, Tunbridge Wells

Cat

The bright, yellow eyes switched back and forth
Its claws sprang out silently
Something moved, its head twitched round
The mouse passed without a sound
Its fur itched the head shot round
And licked thoroughly with its warm, rough tongue
A light flickered on, small feet walked past
It started to purr as the hand stroked hard
Then she left and it shot back to its senses
The fridge was open, what a pleasant surprise
It crept so slowly, the Sunday roast smelled inviting
And reached up high, but could not reach
It tried and tried, but still not yet
It gave up trying; its eyes picked up on a little squeak
It turned round slowly and . . .
Pounced!

Samantha McCall (11)
Bennett Memorial Diocesan School, Tunbridge Wells

Greyhound

Their hearts beating like Death's drum
Nails blunt and minds dumb.
The blackness of a greyhound's heart is nothing.
Their mouths open and their tongues hang out
As the crowd start to cheer and shout.
The traps open and out they run
Bright-eyed and happy, under the hot sun.
Their only thoughts are food and sleep.
The dogs' feet fly across the ground
They see everything but hear hardly a sound.
The gamblers sit in high chairs
Fixed on those hounds are all their cares.
To the end the race is won by Enola-Gay!

Rachel Dawson (11)
Bennett Memorial Diocesan School, Tunbridge Wells

The Game

Today there is a big game, a football game you know
Larkfield Juniors vs Blue Eagles, I am in it, come on let's go!
In the changing rooms, home and away
The managers are giving their plans and the players ready to play!

On we walk, the crowd is cheering and chanting
'C'mon Larkfield! C'mon Juniors! You can *win!*'
The captains shake hands, quickly breaking grip
The referee has the coin and now it's starting to flip.

Eagles kick-off, passing the ball out wide
Robbie, one of our defenders has to slide
His challenge was fair and he cleared up the pitch
I, the striker, ran onto it and passed it back to Mitch.

Mitch shot, it was curling in
But the keeper saved and it hit the post with a din
I sprinted past the defenders onto the loose ball
But a big defender ran into me, I thought I'd hit a wall!

Free kick! The ref brings out the red card
I step to take the shot, this could be very hard
I look at my target, left or right?
The final minute comes, I'm trembling like mad, I look a sight.

I make my decision, I start my run up
The ball flies, the keeper dives, into the top right hand corner is the ball
We have done it! We've won the cup!
Now Larkfield Juniors stand tall!

James Smith (11)
Bennett Memorial Diocesan School, Tunbridge Wells

Starting A Fire

Wood and coal is brought from outside
To be put in the car for its bumpy ride!

When it's brought home, it's left alone
Sitting on a pile of ash.

Then later on the wood hears someone coming,
But they're not just coming, they're really running.

'That's him,' the wood said, 'it's the children's dad.
He burns us to death, he's really bad!'

He lit a match in front of them
The wood went to his children in their den.

'He's here now,' the wood said, 'you've got to come out.
For he's opened the box and the match is about.'

They both came out to see a bright flame
The wood's children said, 'At our funeral, he'll be to blame.'

He lit their newspaper which burned them alive
They all just wanted to go and hide.

They all caught fire and joined their friends
Underneath the fire where everything ends.

But the fire still blazed, orange, yellow and red
It seemed it didn't care whether anyone was dead.

Rebecca Johnson (12)
Bennett Memorial Diocesan School, Tunbridge Wells

Snow

It's snow secret
I love snow
Days off school
Hours of fun
Snow fights
Sledging down hills
Wish I could go faster
Building igloos
Making snowmen
Standing up in a blizzard
Catching snowflakes on my tongue
Temperature's below freezing
Hats, gloves and scarves
Try and keep warm
I love snow
It's snow secret!

Peter King (12)
Bennett Memorial Diocesan School, Tunbridge Wells

My Poem

Wiggly fingers
Fuzzy hair
Pudgy face
Little toes
Bulky belly
Sparkling eyes
Rose red lips
Cherry cheeks
And tiny nose.

Laura Russell (12)
Bennett Memorial Diocesan School, Tunbridge Wells

Alien Invasion

People running
People screaming
People crying
People dying
All this happens when the aliens invade
They say there is a debt to be paid.

Windows smashing
Cars crashing
The power is out, including the lighting
But the army is still loyally fighting
All this happens when the aliens invade
They say there is a debt to be paid.

Earth is lost
The aliens have won
The alien rule has begun!

Patrick Osborn (12)
Bennett Memorial Diocesan School, Tunbridge Wells

Words

What are words?
Only a bunch of mixed up letters
What are letters?
Lines put in different places
Why are they there?
So . . . people can talk
So people can speak
So people can write
So people can read
So I can write this poem
And
So that you can read it!

Annie Moore (12)
Bennett Memorial Diocesan School, Tunbridge Wells

Life

Is there a Heaven and Hell?
Is life black and white or both together one long stretch of grey?
Is there a beginning and an end?
Is life good or bad?
Is life mostly perfect white, but turned into cream by a hint of
spitting yellow?
Is life just how you take it?
Is there even a colour?
Is there a meaning to every different person?
Is life nothing?
Is life simply sky-blue?

Catherine Spreadbury (11)
Bennett Memorial Diocesan School, Tunbridge Wells

War

Sitting in the dark
Nothing there to see
Cold, wet and sick
No one's nursing me.

Bombs are going off
Cracking on the ground
Houses falling down
My head is spinning round.

Families are all dying
Something's going wrong
Everyone is fighting
It's going on too long.

Sitting by myself
No one there for me
Lonely in the rubble
Why can't people see?

Rachel Dunlop (11)
Bennett Memorial Diocesan School, Tunbridge Wells

German Shepherds

G erman shepherds are sleek
E ars that are upright
R uns so fast like a cheetah
M ainly happy, but sometimes moan
A nd sometimes they are loving
N ow they can also be obedient

S o when you're feeling lonely
H er face will always cheer you up
E ager to be with you
'P lease stroke me!' she says
H er coat is so soft
E ven though she can get angry
R espect your dog
D o, because you know the dog will always love you.

Amie Roberts (12)
Bennett Memorial Diocesan School, Tunbridge Wells

Spring Clean

S ponges out
P rimroses blossoming
R eady to clean
I get ready
N ever know what to do
G oing to shops to buy soap

C ountry houses are clean
L ook inside at the cleanness
E ating outside in the sun
A sponge or two
N ow dirty.

Alice Burrell (12)
Bennett Memorial Diocesan School, Tunbridge Wells

The Ocean

The ocean is creating wild waves
That wash up pebbles on the beach
The ocean is creating wild waves
That brighten up rocks better than bleach.

The ocean is a home for many creatures
That hide in rocks or sand
The ocean is a home for many creatures
Fighting the current to stay on land.

The ocean is hit by massive storms
That strand many fish
The ocean is hit by massive storms
That build up whirlpools shaped like a dish.

The ocean is a very fascinating place
That anyone can love
The ocean is a very fascinating place
That I think is better than the heavens above.

Rohan Thorniley (11)
Bennett Memorial Diocesan School, Tunbridge Wells

Shipwreck

The sea was calm
Taking a breath before the storm
Then it let go of the breath.

Suddenly the sailors were caught off guard
A few were thrown overboard.

Then the ship, without warning, gave way upon the rocks
Wood splintered and shattered around
Within minutes the ship was wiped from the face of the Earth.

David Taylor (12)
Bennett Memorial Diocesan School, Tunbridge Wells

Earthquake

Every earthquake likes to strike fear
To people's eyes they like to bring tears
Every moment could be your last
So watch out for the after-shocking blast.

Buildings crumble to the ground
Under the rubble, people are found
Dead bodies lying all over the place
Looking back to the past people just can't face.

People screaming, hoping they're dreaming
The traffic's not moving and nobody's grooving
There are cracks in the road
No one's in a happy mode.

Then the ground stops shaking
The unconscious start awaking
It's all over
There's nothing left but a little red Rover.

Anna Brown (11)
Bennett Memorial Diocesan School, Tunbridge Wells

Cheese!

Cheese is creamy, cheese is fun
Lots of cheese, all day long

Cheddar's better than ordinary cheese
It's made in Cheddar, give me some please!

Cheeses, cheeses I love them all
Lots of cheese, here I come!

Stephen Cheeseman (12)
Bennett Memorial Diocesan School, Tunbridge Wells

Mount Doom

The fiery volcano, Mount Doom
Stands high, towering the little town St Clune
The glowing rock can burn through the strongest steel
It can burn through human skin, which no doctor can heal
There was once a story told by the townspeople
That there lived a man in Mount Doom, who had worked in the church's steeple
He lived on his own, not speaking to a soul
All he owned was a bed, a chair, a spoon and a bowl
But one terrible day, with frightened faces, they said
The man turned into a fire-breathing dragon with claws like lead
His eyes glowed like fire, his teeth were like razor knives
He killed anyone in his path, taking so many people's lives
But one scary night last year in June
The townspeople were celebrating the full moon
He came rampaging to their party, ruining all their fun
He killed the town mayor and his wife, but then disappeared
                                        before the morning sun
No one knows where he is and they keep asking why
And the town children are not sure whether it's true or a lie
No one knows what happened that day
'He is still out there,' as some people say!

Isabelle Darque (12)
Bennett Memorial Diocesan School, Tunbridge Wells

The Blind Man

'Why?' is the question that the blind man asked
As he walked across the pearly moonlit grass
He could not see the trees so green
All he could picture was the war he had seen
He got to the shore praying that the war would be done
And drowned himself under the rising sun.

Joseph Cherry (12)
Bennett Memorial Diocesan School, Tunbridge Wells

My Pets

Fluffy is my cat
He is very fat
He runs around rarely
He is very hairy
He's black and white
He loves to fight
He eats and eats and eats and eats
That's all he does all day

Nibbles is my bunny
He is very funny
He eats lots of bread
And loves to be fed
He runs to and fro
And bites my big toe
He runs and runs and runs and runs
That's all he does all day.

Sarah Matchett (11)
Bennett Memorial Diocesan School, Tunbridge Wells

Friends

Friends are always there for you
And I'm always there for them too
I can trust them anyway
I listen to things they do and say
I can have a great big laugh
All of us together are really daft
Like putting milkshake in each other's hair
And throwing food everywhere
But our main friends are our families
I think you definitely would agree with me.

Rebecca Taylor (12)
Bennett Memorial Diocesan School, Tunbridge Wells

Winnie The Pooh - A Flood In The Hundred Acre Wood

It was a terrible day when the river was high
Winnie thought he was going to die
He made a honeypot into a boat
Winnie said, 'I hope it will float'

It was rainy and cloudy, certainly not sunny
But Winnie the Pooh was happy in his pot of honey
All his full pots of honey floated away
Winnie hoped they'd come back another day

All his friends were upset and sad
They'd never seen weather so bad
Rabbit, Owl, Kanga and Roo
Christopher Robin, Eeyore, Piglet and Tigger too
The rain stopped and the sun came out
Winnie and his friends with happiness did shout:
'Hooray! Hooray! The rain has gone away
Please don't come back for many a day!'

Alice Whittome (11)
Bennett Memorial Diocesan School, Tunbridge Wells

Remember

R emember the soldiers who fought for England
E very single one
M embers of families crying for them
E very tear meaning something
M emories stay with them
B ad ones and good
E veryone all over the world
R emember them always, remember forever.

Sophie Stock (12)
Bennett Memorial Diocesan School, Tunbridge Wells

My Land Of Dreams

Alarm clock screaming monsters drag me from my land of dreams
Though I would sooner stay there where nothing is as it seems
Where I can feel some peace of mind
Where the people all are kind

But I once again must face the world
Be forced to feel alone and cold
Where I can feel no peace of mind
Where the people are not kind

This life we lead is overrated
People are discriminated
Where we can feel no peace of mind
Where the people are not kind

Then I hear the school bell ring
Its sharp sounds cut and sting
Where I can feel no peace of mind
Where the people are not kind

Along the road I turn and turn
The car is glinting in the sun
Where I can feel no peace of mind
Where the people are not kind

At the squeal of breaks I see a light
And I'm floating upwards like a kite
To where I can feel some peace of mind
To where the people are kind

I drift into my land of dreams
Where nothing is as it seems.

Abigail Rhodes (12)
Bennett Memorial Diocesan School, Tunbridge Wells

The Earthquake

I had the choice
Be silent or scream
I had the choice
But I couldn't make up my devastated mind

If I screamed
The dust would've killed me
If I was silent
No one would have found me

Suddenly I heard a voice
Coming nearer and nearer
It was a man
He found me, he found me

It was my dad
He saved me, he saved me
Then I turned around
And saw the devastation.

Charlotte Wright (11)
Bennett Memorial Diocesan School, Tunbridge Wells

Purple

Purple is a sunset
Purple is a plum
Purple looks like jelly wobbling up and down
Purple is the sky like the morning sun
Purple is the colour of my favourite bubblegum

Purple is the colour of my birthday cake
Purple is the colour of my cuddly snake
Purple is the colour of my bunk bed
Purple is the colour of my scrunchie on my head.

Lauren Cutts (12)
Bennett Memorial Diocesan School, Tunbridge Wells

Sonnet No 1

I saw you standing in the road today
You looked at me, then you smiled and waved too
I waved back but there was a slight delay
We are meant to be together I knew
I kept thinking about you all week long
I really hope you're thinking about me
Maybe you are in love maybe I'm wrong
I think I might invite you in for tea
I invited you, you came round last night
You fell in love with me, I am so glad
I have always wanted to hold you tight
Are we in love or am I going mad?
And we are now in love and together
And this will be forever and ever.

Alex Clipp (12)
Bishopshalt School, Uxbridge

The Beach

The soft waves tumble on the golden sand
Seagulls fly high searching for bits of grub
Once it is spotted they head straight for land
People have a drink in their local pub
The children play with their buckets and spades
They build spectacular golden castles
Flying fish leap up from the gentle waves
Fishermen take out large fish in parcels
Baby crabs scuttle around on the shore
Corals lie at the bottom of the sea
Stingrays rest camouflaged on the sea floor
Children splash one another joyfully
Up in the sky there is a big blue kite
Slowly the sun fades into the still night.

Jayna Chauhan (12)
Bishopshalt School, Uxbridge

Sonnet 100

You fly oh so elegantly up high
Earth must look so weak all the way up there
For your home and your playground is the sky
You can do anything without a care
For you are higher than any mountain
Yet you're quick as a cheetah on patrol
You can flow like a stream or a fountain
Yet as sweet and innocent as a foal
For no one can call themselves your master
You can keep on going with no limit
On and on you go, faster and faster
You are always so tender and timid
What care you take in everything you do
Oh graceful bird, how much I envy you.

Thomas Reed (12)
Bishopshalt School, Uxbridge

Sonnet One

My budgie's squawk is music to my ears
His eyes twinkle like stars in the night sky
His natural beauty is so very clear
His youth and liveliness will never die
His legs are powerful and talons strong
His alert, bright eyes spy your every move
His wings are wide and help him swoop along
But his harmlessness, his nature does prove
Though now his old age is starting to show
His beautiful feathers are falling out
Both hearing and sight beginning to go
He is very tired and wobbles about
But I will forever love him the same
In my memory he'll always remain.

Rachael Collins (12)
Bishopshalt School, Uxbridge

My Sonnet

Even in the darkest of the dark nights
If I am alone or full of deep woe
Just the thought of you and the darks are lights
And that is why I want, need you to know
You are the summer, in my winter cold
Just to be with you, see you, I treasure
We have no past, but our future untold
To know you're near is happy, is pleasure
When I see you in mind, I have to smile
Your laughter is music, song in my heart
To glimpse at you I would walk mile and mile
Your sketches are perfect, beyond great art
Your beauty, your wit and heart are most true
I want you, I need you and I love you.

Rajiv Karia (12)
Bishopshalt School, Uxbridge

The Sky

I love the way you light up bright at night
I love the way you watch me go to sleep
I love the way you wake me very bright
I love the way you never make a peep
I adore the way you rain when I'm sad
I love when planes make white streaks in your eye
I adore it when you shine when I'm glad
You are always happy but sometimes shy
When I look up you make me so jolly
When I look down I give out a big sigh
I adore the way you melt my lolly
I wish I could touch you, but you're too high
I will love you forever and ever
I and you must always be together.

Taranjit Rai (12)
Bishopshalt School, Uxbridge

Sea Stretch

I can see the sea, stretching far away for miles,
The air has a taste of salt sticking like glue to my tongue,
The sprays of water taste gritty, sharp and salty.
The sun like a glittery, glazing disco ball, high in the sky.

While the water feels fresh, free and fast against my legs,
You feel the odd, sharp, painful pinch from a crazy crab,
See fish jumping, joyfully out of people's hands,
While you can hear the seagulls squawking up above.

Sparkling, glowing, glinting shells, left along the sandy shore,
The sand is the colour of pure white snow.
The air smells of slippery, smelly fish all through the day,
Whilst the sun is gently dying down, low.

Abbie Palmer (13)
Broadstone Middle School, Broadstone

A Ghost Poem

The wind, ghostly and quiet,
Then a scream on the air,
The galloping of hooves,
Oh horror!
The headless rider,
The rushing of feet,
My clammy hands,
Hairs on my back . . . prickle!
Oh horror!
My heart hammering,
He's coming closer,
The stumble of feet,
A glint of a hint of my doom,
A flash of light,
The solid floor,
Oh hor . . .

Oliver Timmis (12)
Broadstone Middle School, Broadstone

Land Of The Rising Sun

In the land of the rising sun
The purifying light kills all evil beasts.
The chimera, the Minotaur and the harpy
Are vanquished and the Samurai
Fight no more to defend their village.

In the land of the rising sun
The sun is a radioactive fireball
Turning cloud to a candyfloss carousel
And the sky into a fierce furnace,
Fiercer and brighter than ordinary fire.

In the land of the rising sun
The sun is a saint rising over the horizon
Marching to liberate us from Hell and our demise.
The sun is life and the living,
Rising in the east and setting in the west.

In the land of the rising sun
The sun burns all people who go out at midday
And boils all fish in the seas and rivers.
The sun is as light as a gaslight newly lit,
In a dark and desolate world without meaning,
In the land of the rising sun.

David Musselwhite (13)
Broadstone Middle School, Broadstone

The Clown - Haiku

Here's the evil clown
His smile is like a melon
Green and pitiful

Multicoloured face
It's worse than the bearded girl
Ugly and twisted.

Daniel Wakefield (13)
Broadstone Middle School, Broadstone

The Fireball

The blistering days of striking sun that forms millions of
Smiles all around. The ball of light that
Makes the skies furnace in heat throughout the
Days and through the night.

The blinding eyes, the blue skies.
The running children the burning dies.
The scorching deserts, the windy days
These are the days people do it their own way.

The weather is hot, the time is right
Come outside and see the sight
The day is ending the sun is falling
The children stop shouting and calling.

The sunset ends, the stars start to appear
The sun is gone and the night is here
It's been a day to remember of joy and happiness
The silence I hear, the next day is near.

Paige Edwards (12)
Broadstone Middle School, Broadstone

The Sea

The beautiful sunrise to start off the day,
Waking up to see the silky, soft sandy beach.
The rushing, splashing waves crashing on the seabed,
As fast as a cheetah.

The slimy fish jumping joyfully out of the salty, cold, rocky water.
The shuffling crabs scatter quickly scurrying for food.
Screaming children, ice cream cornets, seagulls squeaking.
Seashells in a fabulous line drifting across the water.
From the lovely reflection of the sun.

Seaweed sliding beneath the cold, wet feet of children
The crashing waves toppling onto the rough rock pools.
To finish the day off, a gorgeous sunset to signal night.

Heather O'Brien (13)
Broadstone Middle School, Broadstone

Through A Fox's Eyes

Why me?
It is life,
To hunt, to live,
It's not my fault I have to eat,
Why should I suffer to feed my needs?

Horses charge, dogs snarl, hooves crush,
My life in danger, my paws scamper,
The vicious dogs snap at me,
You have to eat,
So do I,
Why me?

Fun,
Not for me,
Selfish humans,
Murder me, and my family,
You make many orphans in my life,
You cry when you lose someone close,
That's what we do; we are not invincible to feelings,

An enjoyable sport is what you call this brutal murder,
Fox-hunting in my eyes is like me hunting you,
You would not like it, would you?
I certainly don't.
Tasty chicken,
I have to eat,
Why me
?

Emily Magnus (12)
Broadstone Middle School, Broadstone

By The Sea

For me, in the summer,
Where I love to go,
Is down by the seaside,
With my family in tow.

Trudging down the chine,
Bright surfboards on our backs,
Buckets, spades and beach balls,
Picnic in a rucksack.

Splashing in the cold sea,
Squeals of pure delight,
Out comes the volleyball,
We dive left and right.

We dig ourselves a great big hole,
The bottom's nice and flat,
From inside all sound is muffled,
As if wearing a woolly hat.

Collecting shells is great fun,
Sometimes crabs as well,
We try to avoid seaweed,
Because it's such a smell.

A football kicked back and forth,
Slowing as it hits the lumps,
We're all sandy, *in the sea!*
The chill gives me goosebumps.

We're offered ice cream and set off home,
I'm feeling rather sad,
Mum says, 'Don't worry, we'll be back tomorrow.'
That makes me rather glad!

David Iles (12)
Broadstone Middle School, Broadstone

The World I Live In

The world I live in is barren and remote,
With chilli reds, cumin yellows, saffron brown, sizzling sweltering heat
Lying back on an array of soft silk cushions,
Mesmerised by the timid breeze,
That gently teases the tent flaps open,
Allowing the calls of the other Nomadic herders to float in,
Accompanying the spicy aroma of *asida*, Mama's speciality,
That simmers slowly under the shady sand dunes,
Which tower over the children playing *arikkia* in the midday sun.

The world I live in is wild and free,
Trickling crystal streams, velvet moss, snow-capped mountains,
Soaring sycamores shadow our log cabin,
Autumn brings berries, nuts, pumpkins and potatoes,
Plentiful profusion of every food,
Animals and birds building up stocks for the harsh winter,
Drifts of dazzling, gleaming, sparkling, pearly snow,
Like the masses of fragrant blossom in spring.

The world I live in is grey and dull,
Cramped and noisy,
In this colossal, dismal block of flats,
Clogged with the stench of vomit,
Confounded with shrieks, bangs, wails, yells and the
                                    main road to London,
I clamber to the summit to squint into the sunset horizon,
In sight of a better world,
Where I can play properly,
Where my family won't be carelessly tossed away like rubbish,
Into homes of bedlam.

Helena Kipling (11)
Broadstone Middle School, Broadstone

Wings

Under my wings I'll see the earth that everything lies on,
Trees in their coats of emerald-green leaves,
Are swaying in the wind as they dance,
People are scurrying between the buildings as I fly over the busy city,
A patchwork of umbrellas is made in the drizzling rain,
Beneath my wings.

Under my wings you'll find animals of every sort,
From tiny mice with little, pink, beady eyes,
To enormous blue whales with tails like motors,
To push them powerfully through the sea,
Yes, a lot below my wings is that turquoise water,
But deserts also roam here and there,
Covered in their sandy grains,
Beneath my wings.

Under my wings we'll gaze upon castles and palaces
                                    in all their splendour,
Farmers' fields filled with crops to grow and feed on,
Countryside meadows littered with wild flowers,
That have a delightful odour,
Roads scribbled on the ground where the endless speed of cars
Can be heard from all around,
Beneath my wings.

Deborah Smith (12)
Broadstone Middle School, Broadstone

Sea And Lightning

The rough waters of the sea
Chopping and smacking
The beach once full of people.

The smashing thunder slashing
The ground with pace
The yellow flash, amazing.

Timothy Wilcock (13)
Broadstone Middle School, Broadstone

A Word From The Tiger

You humans, always rushing around,
Getting where you need to go.
My life couldn't be more different,
I prefer to take things slow.

I have time to ponder the world,
To think of how I came to be,
I cannot do this all the time,
I have to hunt, as you will see.

I am king of my domain,
And as I hunt, the animals flee,
They know that I can kill them all,
And they expect no less of me.

I have inspired generations,
Warriors, poets and tribes,
My power is legendary,
And hippies like my vibes.

And yet you humans want me dead,
You shoot, you trap, you dam.
What did I do to anger you?
Except be what I am.

Cara Little (12)
Broadstone Middle School, Broadstone

Easter Egg Hunt

The Easter Bunny comes overnight,
He leaves chocolate eggs as a sign of delight,
The Easter egg hunt is about to begin,
So huddle around, it's time to dig in,
Look everywhere you go children,
As they are hidden in the undergrowth,
Or maybe up a tree,
But do it quite quickly,
As it's nearly time for tea.

Madeleine Allam (11)
Broadstone Middle School, Broadstone

My Pencil Case

Look in my pencil case with sheer delight,
Some savoured chewing gum, what a fright!

Inky tissues and pens that leak,
Secret messages I dare not speak!

A cartridge pen full of ink,
I wait to write down what I think!

Tissues green and full of snot,
Pieces of homework, I think not!

Elastic toggles to tie up my hair,
Make-up not allowed, that's not fair!

Children whispering, rubbers flying,
Teachers teaching, new friends meeting!

Look in my pencil case with sheer delight,
Savoured chewing gum, what a fright!

Amelia McDougal (11)
Broadstone Middle School, Broadstone

Sunshine

The sun enters over the morning sea,
A burning fire rises and shimmers,
Piercing the blistering people below,
Mellow yellow sunshine.

Shimmering sun, glinting over the shiny sea,
Mirroring the rising sun,
Blinding whiteness,
Water calms.

The people start to drift away,
Suncream disappears,
The sun slowly slides through the clouds,
But still the sly sun burns.

Jerry Trotter (12)
Broadstone Middle School, Broadstone

On The Beach

The red-hot scorching sun,
Sizzles my cells one by one.
I take a drink from my can,
But then I'm shaded by a big fat man.

Some kids playing in the sea,
Others end up playing by me!
They kick sand in my face,
As they run by me at a speedy pace.

I have to stop and stare,
As I look at that lifeguard over there.
I search my bag,
For my mag,
Which I finally find.
Ouch! My eyes, the sun is making me go blind.

The boiling sand burns my feet,
I'm not sure I'll be back next week.

Anna Williams (11)
Broadstone Middle School, Broadstone

The Blazing Sun

The sun is sinking into the misty, blue water,
The blazing, bright sky is as rosy as pink candyfloss,
The terracotta sun is floating down, like a feather to the ground,
The clouds are like pure, pearly-white, cotton wool.

The blistering sun burns my tanned skin to a flaming red colour,
I stare at the sun but it blinds my eyes.
I close them and think of the next day to come,
The scorching sun is like a bright, white light bulb.

The sun exits the golden coloured sky and disappears,
To another part of our glorious world.
Visiting different countries, showing off its blinding beams;
Spectacular colours of the day.

Hayley Ansell (13)
Broadstone Middle School, Broadstone

Footy Crazy

Volley it, chip it
Over here . . . shoot!
Juggle it, flick it
Drill it with your boot!

Thump it, swerve it
Down the wing . . . pass!
Dribble it, head it
That was so class!

Mark up, skin 'im
Watch out for the ref!
Blast it, curl it
Whack it in the net!

Wallop it, whip it
Winning five goals to four!
Hammer it, pelt it
Ref's whistle, final score!

Damien Longdin (13)
Broadstone Middle School, Broadstone

Scared

Heart stopping
Teeth rattling
Neck biting
Doom wishing
Scared screaming
Brain teasing
Doors banging
Life ending
Death carrying
Blood freezing
Bone mashing
Vampire.

James Bissell (12)
Broadstone Middle School, Broadstone

Sunshine

The sun in the morning starts to appear
Over the horizon,
A powerful energy ball.
Rays of the sun
As gold as jewels,
Scorching sun sizzles in mid-air.

The sun in the afternoon climbs high
Over the meadows;
A ball of fire,
As hot as lava.
The clouds, like rabbits' tails,
The spectacular sun races with the moon.

Grace Simpson (12)
Broadstone Middle School, Broadstone

Spy

I run through the bushes, dark and wet,
No time to watch the fiery sunset.
I reach the door, lock-pick in hand,
A click, a scratch, and I'm out of this land.
I walk towards the glow of a building,
From inside, I hear a gentle, *ping!*
I take the lock-pick out again,
I open the door as it starts to rain.
Inside the plant, my heartbeat racing,
I take the Semtex out of its casing.
The fragile det cord, long and thin,
I light the fuse and plug it in.
I stick the explosive to the door,
I run away and count to four.
'One, two, three, four!'
Bang!

Jordan Tomkins (12)
Broadstone Middle School, Broadstone

On The Beach In The Sun

The trill of a coastguard's whistle,
And the cries of annoyed sunbathers,
As they get sand in their eyes,
And the thump, thump, thump of a beach ball being kicked around,
This is the orchestra of my beach sounds.

The sea shines like polished metals,
The field of multicoloured umbrellas and an occasional tent,
The newly built sandcastles, crushed like petals,
The last bit of money on ice cream's spent,
This is the photo of my beach sights.

Elliott Bailey (12)
Broadstone Middle School, Broadstone

The Dream

I lay back, close my eyes,
And dream back to a bright sunny day.
Where the dancing horses lap the lonely shore,
The sea air hits me, then I remember more,
Angelfish swim and dolphins dive and leap,
I wish I could return here everyday of the week,
The pretty pearled shell glitter in the sunlight,
Then the sun goes down and in creeps night,
So the magical sea creatures disappear,
The moon smiles down at me;
It looks so near.
I reach out to the stardust,
I sit in awe,
Then milky rays hit the silent shore.
The moon sinks; the sun starts to rise,
A spectrum of colours fills the skies.
It's a beautiful sight,
But I turn away,
And open my eyes to another day.

Sofia Protopsaltis (13)
Broadstone Middle School, Broadstone

The Bog

Shivering, damp and full of dread,
The line up waits in fear.
For some the chance to prove their worth,
For me a low spot in the year.

It's time to take on nature's test
Of bramble, mud and fog.
It's time to see if lungs and legs
Can lift you from the bog.

Cross-country team in blue and black
Are poised to hear the sound
That starts the race and makes your heart
Begin to swell and pound.

We're off with arms and legs flung wide,
A lap of field before the gate,
Then heath and sand and mud
That stretch of earth you love to hate.

Down the slopes, up the hills,
Through the grabbing gorse.
We force ourselves to forge ahead
On the school's cross-country course.

And now with chest and legs on fire
The bog is just ahead,
An endless stretch of salty pool
That fills us all with dread.

I plunge my feet into the mire,
And sink down to my waist.
I pull my feet up as best I can,
While others pass in haste.

I force myself to swim the rest
And find that I've got through.
I think I'm still in one whole piece,
But only with one shoe.

Alex Wathen (12)
Broadstone Middle School, Broadstone

The Titanic

It happened on April the tenth
Away, away it went by noon
With 2227 passengers and crew,
Sailing to their doom.

The ship was beautiful as it faded away
Perfectly streamlined, it was on its way
'Congratulations, congratulations,' came from other ships
'Warnings of icebergs ahead,' from other lips

The weather was beautiful
Peaceful and calm,
Her speed went up,
Next, the crew sounded the alarm.

'Warning, warning, slight hazes ahead!'
Then the message came, 'large iceberg nears'
'Hard a starboard,' the officer said.
A 300-foot hole in the bottom appears,
'The Titanic is sinking,' the passengers hear.

The lifeboats are uncovered
Who won't see tomorrow?
'Women and children first!' officers cry,
For they know many will die.

The Carpathian picks up remaining survivors,
Warm clothes, hot soup
But only for the divers
The Titanic, with passengers, sinks to the ground.

Yasmin Dunnett (11)
Broadstone Middle School, Broadstone

The Seasons

Spring
The first bird tweeting its first tune of the year,
Is as wonderful to hear as a baby's first word.
The blossoming flowers are as beautiful,
As a rainbow being touched by the sunlight.
The pleasant weather brightens everyone up,
Like new toys do to very little children.
The young lambs waddling for the first time brings tears to eyes,
Like hearing a new family member has been born.
This is why spring is so great

Summer
The glorious summer sun felt wonderful,
As if paradise would keep on going forever.
The beach umbrella shielded the scolding sun
As a sword would defend a soldier.
The buzzing bees danced around the garden joyfully,
As if they were at a party.
The sand at the seaside was being dug up by small children,
As if they were hoping to find Australia.
That is why summer is so great.

Autumn
The sunset was as vibrant as fire,
Bearing every shade of red, orange and yellow.
The sky was as blue as the ocean,
Bearing all sorts of wonderful exotic creatures.
The grass was as moist and chilling as a snowball,
Melting in the palms of children's hands.
The leaves were rustling along the road,
As schoolgirls would, if they had a new secret to share.
This is why autumn is so great.

Winter
The snow settled and melted on the ground,
Like butter on freshly made toast.
The chilling wind whistled through the trees,
Like someone remembering a song.
The branches from the oak tree,
Looked like a deserted playground; empty.
The ice on the pavement was as shiny as a window
That has been scrubbed minutes ago.
That is why winter is so great.

Natalie Grew (12)
Broadstone Middle School, Broadstone

Through My Eyes

If you look through my eyes and into a mirror
You will see someone fake
Someone telling a lie to the world
The spotlight glares, as millions of people
Watch an actress out of a very real play;
Like a chameleon I change -
I am myself for a moment;
I am happy for a short while
On goes the foundation, the blusher,
Mascara and lipstick altering my appearance;
Standing in my place, is a horrible woman
Driven to be like this through newspapers and magazines,
Telling me I'm 'too fat', 'too slim',
My hair looks awful or 'I love your hair'!

I am trapped in a world of stages, cameras, sets and rumours
I am enclosed in a prison
The fame choking me, killing me slowly . . .
I have to get out, but contracts bind my hands and feet
I realise, I know deep in my heart
That I will never escape from what I thought was a dream come true.

Hannah Washbrook (12)
Broadstone Middle School, Broadstone

The Match

The stadium is full, it's Saturday again,
The crowd wait for the appearance of 22 men,
There's green and yellow, red and white,
Football strips, a match is in sight.

The ball stands still, the whistle blows,
The roar of the crowd quickly grows,
Leather kicks leather, see mud fly,
As the black and white ball flashes by.

The ball is passed from man to man,
The away team tackles if it can,
The ball's near the net, things are tense,
It overshoots and hits the fence.

Another tackle, a header, a kick,
Where's the defender? They must be quick,
The ball sails past, missing wide,
'Sack the ref, the player's offside'.

The crowd all groan, score is nil-nil,
But the star player shows his skill,
The ball comes to him in a smooth roll,
Take aim, a kick, and it's a goal.

Matt Cole (12)
Broadstone Middle School, Broadstone

Fire

Fire, the untamed dragon,
The dragon of searing heat, pain and danger,

Fire, scorching the sky itself,
Painting everything black, red, orange and grey,

Black are the houses like the Grim Reaper's cape,
Red is the sky stained as if with boiling blood,

Orange is the sun blazing bright trying to save the day,
Grey is the smoke covering the sky like creeping shadows,

Fire, the tamed dragon
The dragon of warmth, light and safety,

Fire, staying where it is put,
Painting all corners of the room red, orange, black and yellow,

Red is an amazing sunset stretching as far as the eye can see,
Orange is a little child's room, like his heart, it is bright,

Yellow are the curtains he always looks through,
Black the colour of the sky at night like the coal when
the light has gone out.

Fire, the unpredictable dragon,
The dragon that can change our lives with the flare of a match.

Sally Megan Maric (12)
Broadstone Middle School, Broadstone

My Memory As An Evacuee

The 1st of February was the day it happened,
My brother and I were sent away,
To an abnormal place far, far away,
Lots of hills I must say.
Confused, scared, numb with fear.
'What will happen to my dear?'

What are these tags for?
Do they not know my name?
And what's in this bag?
Everyone has the same.
Confused, scared, numb with fear.
'What will happen to my dear?'

Someone's taking me away!
Now they're after my brother!
I hope they don't split us up!
Oh I do miss my mother.
Confused, scared, numb with fear.
'What will happen to my dear?'

My new mother is round and jolly,
She took me through a muddy track,
An enormous dog I think was a collie,
Came bounding towards me, I fell on my back.
Confused, scared, numb with fear.
'What will happen to my dear?'

A house standing by itself?
A picturesque flowery front garden?
To my right there are trees,
I had not seen these.
Confused, scared, numb with fear.
'What will happen to my dear?'

I'm lucky I don't have to work on a farm,
Unlike some of the evacuees,
I just play in the garden
And sometimes I can be lazy.
Coping well, nothing to fear,
'What has happened to my dear?'

The German bombers sadly came
And blitzed our old home,
But Mother wrote she is fine
And is in a brand new home.
Coping well, nothing to fear,
'What has happened to my dear?'

Months have passed, war at end
I've learnt a lot, and been OK,
Can't wait to go home,
In this month of May.
Coping well, nothing to fear,
'What has happened to my dear?'

I'm back in my new home safe and sound,
But where I used to live is flattened to the ground.
Unfortunately good friends have died,
Thank God I'm still alive!

Elysia Pike (12)
Broadstone Middle School, Broadstone

The Wind

The wind surged through the branches,
It picked off all the leaves,
It pulled up all the flowers,
And trembled all the trees.

The wind rattled all the windows,
It shook the garden gate,
It battered all the fences,
And broke the garden rake.

The wind is dying down now,
Its destruction we shall see,
Its line of devastation;
Holds fate for you and me.

Emma Christopher (11)
Broadstone Middle School, Broadstone

All The Fun At Gymnastics

Spinning,
Twisting,
Rotating,
Landing,
All the fun at gymnastics
Flipping,
Somersaulting,
Jumping,
Bouncing,
All the fun at gymnastics
Presenting,
Climbing,
Lifting,
Holding,
All the fun at gymnastics
Stretching,
Cartwheeling,
Leaping,
Tumbling,
All the fun at gymnastics.

Lloyd Mitchener (11)
Broadstone Middle School, Broadstone

Ocean!

The
Beautiful
Boat gleefully
Roaming across
The shining sparkling
Sea. The sea glistens
As the sun's beaming
Rays shimmer down
Onto the immaculate white
Sides of the boat. The gentle
Tide comes pushing light blue
Ripples against the shore. The blue
Lining looks greatly at rest when in
Contact with land. Sand feels so
Fine and calming as the sensational
Tide meets with the remarkably clean
Sand. I sail away from the motionless
Coast and away from the tranquil
Touch of the ocean. My ears
Are in Heaven at the sound
Of diamond-like waves;
Like the sun on a
Cloudy, misty, day.

Cheryl Moss (13)
Broadstone Middle School, Broadstone

Thoughts

In soundless silence
I think to myself,
Thoughts of sadness and joy,
Come to my mind.

I think of a young child,
Full of ambition and hope;
No tears are shed over broken dreams,
A smile is always showing on a child,
Now a smile is showing on me.

I think about poverty;
Guilt comes over me like a looming fog.
No food they eat,
No water they drink,
No love or care,
No hope they receive.

I think of a rainforest,
Full of lush olive-greens,
Water trickling from leaf to leaf,
Then I hear bulldozers,
And machines,
Tearing up trees,
Confusions springs to mind.

I think of all these things,
Some are sad,
Others full of hope.
This is our world,
Filled with both hope and sadness.

Hannah Price (12)
Broadstone Middle School, Broadstone

A New World!

Swim under ocean blue,
Through coral reefs,
A world that's new!

Beneath the waves a calm world lies,
You take a look,
With wide-open eyes.

In a daydream you float around,
Silence surrounds you,
In a fish's playground.

The sun glitters across the sea,
You've unlocked the door to a new world,
With your underwater key.

You swim deeper, deeper down,
You're king of the ocean,
With your seaweed crown.

Rising slowly to take a breath,
You feel revived,
Like life after death.

Diving down, heavy as lead,
Getting faster, deeper,
Your fears are fed.

But my bubble is soon to burst,
Back to my world,
Can't I explore this world first?

Amy Shepherd (12)
Broadstone Middle School, Broadstone

The Model

She finds a beautiful girl staring back at her
When she looks in the mirror.
As she walks down the black, slippery, catwalk,
Her make-up sticks to her face, it smells sweet and sickly,
A sweet scent of flowers flows through her dressing room,
People wait outside for pictures and autographs.

Her mirror is her only friend;
Cold and silver reflects her icy beauty.
Her mask-like face,
Pretty and painted.
Her red lips curl into a meaningless smile.
The mirror's light glitters in her eyes
But no fire flickers,
For the model is as cold as the mirror,
Her heart frozen.

Ellie Thomas (11)
Broadstone Middle School, Broadstone

The Weather!

Sometimes it rains then it stops,
It comes with hail that falls in drops,
Sometimes it's sunny, then it's dark,
It comes with the clouds in the shape of an arc.

Sometimes it's misty then it will fade,
It comes with fog and drifts into shade,
Sometimes it snows, and then it melts,
It comes with gravity so it belts.

Sometimes there's a rainbow, then it's gone
It comes with the rain and where the sun has shone.
After a weathery day, it comes to an end
Here come the darkness and the moon's trend!

James Palmer (12)
Broadstone Middle School, Broadstone

Autumn Walk

Crocus and crimson leaves crackle underfoot,
The path is plastered with crispy foliage.
The smell of new life wafts past my nostrils,
I can hear soft singing birds tweet in the background,
My taste buds tingle as I swallow the fresh air,
I feel a cool breeze brush past my fingertips,
I gaze around;
Children laugh as they sling leaves into the air,
A sudden gust of wind lifts them up into the atmosphere,
Like a hand grasping a ball,
And thrusting it up into the Heavens,
I wander further down the path,
My peach-coloured house is in view,
I turn the key in the lock,
I take one last look at the perfect picture,
Then I step into a world of hustle and bustle.

Katie Neal (11)
Broadstone Middle School, Broadstone

Deep Down

Deep down in the murky depths of the ocean,
The lonely figure of a man lies alone,
His tousled hair swaying in the sea current,
And his pale corpse slowly rotting away.

Deep down in the murky depths of the ocean,
A school of colourful fish swim by,
Cautious of the body below,
Darting in unison quickly past, out of danger.

Deep down in the murky depths of the ocean,
The vibrant spirit of a man rises from the body,
Glowing brightly, lighting up the ocean depths,
Slowly gliding up through the water,
Finally reaching the surface.

Zoe Slater (13)
Broadstone Middle School, Broadstone

My World

(Inspired by 'Prayer Before Birth' by Louis MacNeice)

I'm not yet born,
I would like to be in a world where flowers grow
                                    and birds guide my way.
I'd like to live in the forest where animals seek,
In a cottage roasting my hands by the roaring fire.

I'm not yet born,
I would like to live in a world where people bring peace and care,
Where they do not judge others on their appearance,
                                    religion and hobbies.

I'm not yet born,
Let there be peace
No war, no war.

I'm not yet born,
In my world I wish for clean grass and blue fresh water,
Where fish swim in the sea.

That is the world I'd like to live in
Let no bad thing near me.

Hannah Luxton (11)
Broadstone Middle School, Broadstone

Bonfire Night

Crowds of people huddle around shivering,
    All gazing wide-eyed into the endless sky,
The ink-black curtain was suddenly brought to life,
    With prancing dancing fireworks!
Shooting fireballs explode with showers of light,
    And whirling flames sizzle with rage.
Multicoloured splashes illuminate the dull sky.
    Below the display the bonfire burns,
Full of flickering flames and curling sparks,
    The blazing bonfire seems to hypnotise the spectators.
And the billowing smoke makes their eyes water.
    Like in a war zone, all that is heard are immense explosions,
Ear-piercing shrieks and stunned gasps.

Sparklers fill the empty spaces,
    Flickering in the cool wind like burning stars;
Thrilled toddlers' faces cautiously draw shapes in the air with them.
    Hovering around is the scrumptious scent of warm hot dogs,
Every grinning face is lit up with excitement and joy!
    Having great fun while it lasts as after this
One night, there won't be another display for a whole year.
    The happy faces will soon be tucked up in bed,
As the dazzling display comes to an end.

Sophie Bright (12)
Broadstone Middle School, Broadstone

I Would Like To Be Born In A World

(Inspired by 'Prayer Before Birth' by Louis MacNeice)

I would like to be born in a world of peace,
Without meaningless wars and destruction,
Where weapons don't exist
In a world where the grass is always green
And the wind blows softly.

I would like to be born in a world where the sun is always shining,
And it never rains,
A place where everyone is helpful and nobody ever fights.

I would like to be born in a world where everyone is equal,
There would be food for the whole world,
And there would be cures for every disease.

I would like to be born in a world without terrorism,
In a world with a caring family,
And where no one is not looked after.

I would like to be born in a world of giving and caring for others,
In a world of life and excitement.
In a world where animals are not hunted or
driven out of their habitats.

Jake Elder (11)
Broadstone Middle School, Broadstone

Through My Eyes

If you look at the world through my eyes,
You will see sadness, like clouds of confusion.
Lonely waves of open sea, swirling in the dangerous mists,
Not wanting to step out too far.

If you look at the world through my eyes,
The sun does not shine; the wind does not blow,
The world does not spin.
The small, lively lake is frozen and ill,
And the trees don't wear any leaves to shake in the wind.

If you look at the world through my eyes,
Everything is dying; nothing can grow, like a curse.
The rain is like my cold, turquoise tears.
My sins are too deep,
The scars are too strong, my blood is too cold.

If you look at the world through my eyes,
You would see coffins and bony trees.
As I walk across the lonely path
The leaves crunch like bones under my feet,
I search for a light to forgive me.

If you look at the world through my eyes,
You will see clouds of confusion.

Lauren Hooper (11)
Broadstone Middle School, Broadstone

Alone

All alone, dying slowly
As he lies on the harsh floor;
The rain beating down upon him
The wind whistling through his ears.

All alone, dying slowly
Slumped against the grimy wall,
His forgotten soul weakening
His heart rate pacing low.

All alone, dying slowly
Curled up in a helpless ball,
His bones fragile, crunching
His fearful eyes sinking low.

All alone, dying slowly
Sat amongst the bins,
His scrawny body starving
Whilst his dusty rags blow in the wind.

All alone, dying slowly
He tries to hold on tight,
He lies in despair, saying his goodbyes
As he takes his last, painful breath.

Stephanie Bartlett (12)
Broadstone Middle School, Broadstone

The Shimmering Sea

The sea is light,
As calm as anything,
Drifting quietly,
Rolling its waves onto the hard sand,
Toppling over one another,
Crashing into the seabed.

The sun is slowly disappearing,
Beyond the horizon,
A red, orange and blue sky,
Lighting up the sea,
What's left of the sun?
Sparkles in the distance.

Reflecting onto the shimmering water,
The further you go the deeper it gets,
The deeper you go the colder it gets,
Clouds are drifting,
High in the sky,
The air is slowly getting colder.

A slight breeze,
Hits my face,
Thoughts are filling up in my head,
I feel the air come over me,
Leaping across my face,
My mouth as dry as a desert.

Lauren Troke (12)
Broadstone Middle School, Broadstone

The Night Predator

As the night draws closer and the town falls asleep,
The shadows approach the silent paths
The gas lamps flicker in the brisk wind
And the grass whispers in the moonlight.
Horse and carriage are safely locked away, the town falls silent,
Nothing but the owls can be heard.

As the night falls deeper and the trees fade into the darkness
Of the night, the owls begin their hunt.
The country falls silent at their feet
And the mouse prays for his family's life.
The grasses lay still and the wind stays low;
The night has only just begun.

As the sun wakes up from a peaceful dream
And the moon makes way, a new day is dawning.
The mouse can rest for another day
The sun rises just over the hills and its beautiful colour breaks out;
A new day has arrived.

Beth Clarke (12)
Broadstone Middle School, Broadstone

War

The loud echoing sound of the guns,
The drone of aeroplanes
The cries of wounded men fill my ears.

The large green tanks.
The small determined troops.
The distant enemy, fill my eyes.

The smell of smoke
The smell of fuel
The smell of death, fill my nose

All these thoughts
All these emotions
All these sounds fill my head.

Jack Ingram (13)
Broadstone Middle School, Broadstone

Daydreaming

I try to concentrate on the sums on the jet-black board,
The numbers swirl in front of me, like water going down a plug.
I gaze out of the window and fall into a daydream.
Cotton wool clouds float below me,
I sink into the downy bed.

But my mind wanders like a cave explorer
And suddenly I'm on a football field.
The pitch is as green as emeralds.
It shimmers as the sun beams down onto it.

I run for the ball and strike it hard.
It sails through the air like a boat on the sea.
I go in and the roar of the crowd is like a lion.
I can hear someone calling my name.
I snap back to my senses like fierce crocodile jaws.

My teacher stares back at me, his eyes boring into me.
I pick up my pen and start to scribble . . .

Frances Procter (12)
Broadstone Middle School, Broadstone

Snow

On a hilltop,
It started snowing,
Snowflakes falling,
A breeze was blowing.

Little fluffy faces,
Fill the sky with white,
Twirling, whirling, weaving,
Faces filled with delight.

Red noses are glowing,
The morning has just begun,
The snow won't be here for long,
Because it'll get melted by the sun.

Victoria Frampton (11)
Broadstone Middle School, Broadstone

Through My Eyes

If you look at the world through my eyes,
You will see happiness heaving around the joyful playground,
Tufts of grass flowing and whispering to one another,
Clouds turning jet-black with a breeze in the air.
I watch all the young children scurry inside as the rain pours down,
Drenched little children try to get warm, all wet and cold,
I hold my hair, wringing out the water weighing down my head,
And I wait for the sun to shine, to clear up all the mess it made,
But all I see around me is the sadness that the rain has brought.

If you look at the world through my eyes,
You will see leaping leaves scurrying around,
Nothing being able to grow,
Being eaten away by the lies people say,
Darkened clouds are all around,
Children fighting over the slightest things,
Because the rain has fallen and surrounded them in darkness,
Children don't know how to be kind,
They pick on others and leave them crying, being bullied,
They all come around to the window, everything stops,
The glistening golden sunshine high in the sky once again,
Now people are sweet again, no bullying, no fighting,
They all play together, as a big happy family,
All I can see before my eyes is the happiness,
Heaving around the joyful playground once again on this bright day,
The darkness has left and the brightness has come,
Everyone happy beneath the rainbow.

Vicky West (12)
Broadstone Middle School, Broadstone

Deep Blue Mystery

On the sea's bed the rotting wreck lies,
As if on its deathbed,
It has no disturbance,
Inside it is curious,
Hidden secrets are revealed,
Day by day it is turning to coral,
Covering its motionless body,
Like it is nothing new;
Just part of the deep blue mystery.

Way down under,
It is left alone,
In the cold,
In the dark,
Just lying there, thoughtless,
Maybe waiting to be discovered,
Just part of the deep blue mystery.

Folded in the silken net of the waves,
A glimpse of sunlight just catches the remaining embroidered gold,
Giving off a blinding light,
Like a signal,
As if to say it does not want to be forgotten,
Dissolving away,
Deep down,
Just part of the deep blue mystery.

Jessica Howe (13)
Broadstone Middle School, Broadstone

The Natural World

The natural world has changed, no longer peaceful,
The world it was like a river, steady . . . steady as the beating drum.

The natural world has changed, war has come upon it
Like a boulder on unsteady land, tearing apart, nature destroyed.

The natural world has changed,
The weather forcing us into our homes,
Defacing the land and sea taking the lives of whoever
                                        stands in its way.

The natural world has changed,
More nature being destroyed by evil machines,
Wonderful sealife being polluted by chemical changes.

The natural world has changed, more violence,
More countries fighting, more lives being taken by the fierce weather,
And diseases.

The natural world has changed.

Joshua Horn (13)
Broadstone Middle School, Broadstone

War

There was mayhem,
Gunfire deafened those
Taking part in war
For their countries.

Men screamed in pain
As they were injured,
Slaughtered, explosives destroyed
Vast amounts of lives.

The anti-aircraft guns
Sent planes crash-landing
Into the never-ending
Fields below them.

Suddenly, there was silence.

Adam Mitchell (12)
Broadstone Middle School, Broadstone

Not Yet Born

(Inspired by 'Prayer Before Birth' by Louis MacNeice)

I am not yet born: O hear me.
May my life be peaceful,
May I live in a world where all live in harmony,
And where no dark thoughts will disturb me.

I am not yet born: O hear me.
Let me not be overpowered by the forces of evil,
With their malicious and miserable ways,
Like a dark grey cloud hanging over me.

I am not yet born: O hear me.
Please can I live in a delightful house,
Where dainty flowers blossom before my eyes,
And where I have a family to love and care for me.

Soon I will be born: O hear me.
May I enter the world with my prayer answered.

Jennifer Singleton (12)
Broadstone Middle School, Broadstone

Sea

The gentle waves crash onto the golden sand
Hungry gulls circle looking for food
The sea stretches out beyond the horizon.

There's a world out there under the sea
A world of beauty and delight
A world where there is peace and tranquillity.

The coral sparkles in many colours
The fish swim amongst the fish.

There is no bullying because of size
The sea waves gently crash
Like a raindrop falling into a puddle.

The gentle waves crash onto the golden sand
Hungry gulls circle looking for food
The sea stretches out beyond the horizon.

Robert Ineson (12)
Broadstone Middle School, Broadstone

The Sea

The sea is a fierce lion.
Giant and great and grand and gold.
He guards the beach all day.
With his clamping teeth and whiskered jaws.
Always in charge; watching the boats go by.

Twitching nose, sniffing in the salty ocean smell.
The massive sea lion moans,
Pawing the soft, silky sand.

And when the evening light fades,
And the crescent moon rocks,
He leaps to his feet and roars and roars;
Shaking his soaking side across the rocks,
And purrs and prowls and growls.
Long and low and lonely and loud.

But on quiet days, in May or June,
When even the grasses on the dunes
Rustle no more, their thin high tunes.
With his great maned head
Between his paws,
He rests on the sandy shores.
So calm, so calm he scarcely moves.

Ania Gould (11)
Broadstone Middle School, Broadstone

Snow

Flakes of snow start to fall,
Prettily drifting towards the ground,
Children skate across the lake,
While others sledge down hills,
Frozen white icicles hang from cottage roofs,
Adults put on their woolly hats.

The snow falls faster,
The clouds turn grey,
Children build snowmen,
While adults go inside,
The wind gets colder,
A child cries.

Heavy snow
Starts falling,
Life outside
Soon disappears,
Blizzards blow
The prettiness away.

Andrew Salmon (11)
Broadstone Middle School, Broadstone

Oh What A Woeful War

Soldiers marching to death,
All drunk with fatigue,
No life is spared,
No word is spoken,
Except by the dying soldiers sprawled on the ground,
Their lips move and say; 'Oh! What a woeful war!'

The bitterness of advertising breaks family bonds,
No one smiling,
Children wave goodbye to their fathers,
Mothers mourn for their gullible sons,
The young of fathers sit and stare,
Their lips move steadily and say; 'Oh! What a woeful war!'

The chilly trenches are plagued with disease,
Every soldier is shivering from the draught, no smile is bared,
A tear drops from tired eyes,
They stare blankly at the earthy wall, one phrase is heard;
'Oh! What a woeful war!'

The chalky faces of the dying or dead,
Blood congealed on soldiers' heads,
Their eyes flooded with tears,
All lost with war,
Not proud anymore,
Wishing they were never born,
One sentence is spoken through their blood-covered lips;
'Oh! What a woeful war!'

All is lost, millions dead,
What would happen if we went to war again?

Helen Duyvesteyn (12)
Broadstone Middle School, Broadstone

The Island

The island is quiet,
The only thing to hear,
Is the sound of the waves,
Crashing onto the shore.

Palm trees gently blow in the wind,
A cool breeze is felt,
But the sun still shines,
Making the golden sands glow.

A coconut splashes into the sea,
Breaking the relaxing silence,
Ripples create a pretty pattern,
In the clear, fresh water.

The island is deserted,
The whole world seems silent,
The sandy beaches are empty,
The deep blue sea seems alone.

The day turns into night,
The wind gets up,
The waves get bigger,
The island seems more alone.

The island is never found,
It is paradise,
So wonderful,
Just like a dream.

Hannah Roberts (12)
Broadstone Middle School, Broadstone

Through My Eyes

If you look at the world through my eyes,
You will see crashing waves and silent sands,
Towering palm trees and tropical fish,
Turquoise skies and chalky clouds.
Jade-green trees and delicate lilac flowers.

If you look at the world through my eyes,
You will see old wrinkled men growing crops in the dusty dry fields,
Happy children playing in the long grasses,
Smiling and laughing.
You will smell the fresh lush fruits hanging on the blossom trees.
You will hear calm, soothing music and gentle whistling winds.

You will watch gnarled women collecting water from a stone well
To help their families.
And healthy cattle grazing in the distance.
You will notice young children enjoying school
And caring for their friends and family.

If you look at the world through my eyes
You will see tender, affectionate people.

Charlotte Ivey (12)
Broadstone Middle School, Broadstone

Prayer Before Birth

(Inspired by 'Prayer before Birth' by Louis MacNeice)

P lease let the world be free of war and anger,
E ncourage love and peace to all.
A ppreciate that some of us are good, others bad,
C ancel out racism,
E ncourage people to think.

F orgive the wrongdoers in your world,
O h Lord, take away pain,
R id us of all annoyance.

A cknowledge that some do wrong,
L et us share all our differences,
L et me be proud to be born into your world.

P lease let us be equal,
E xterminate all arguments and stress,
O h Lord, give us hope,
P ut by all of the wickedness and concentrate on goodness,
L et us share your world as one,
E ngage us all in your wonderful world with its canopy
of green and gold.

Dan Pugh (12)
Broadstone Middle School, Broadstone

Sky!

The sky has many moods
They can be of darkness and despair,
Clouds smothering the light,
Like a blanket of evil,
Killing all good.

The sky has many moods
They can be of happiness and joy,
The sun shining on the world,
Like a smile of joy,
Helping and caring.

The sky has many secrets
Secrets of sadness,
Meteorites crashing towards Earth and exploding stars,
Secrets of evil,
Aliens developing weapons and planning invasions.

The sky has many secrets
Secrets of hope,
New planets for us to colonise and capture,
Secrets of joy,
Alien ambassadors coming to give us new technology.

The sky is a place of danger and despair,
But hope still clings on.

Natasha Underwood (11)
Broadstone Middle School, Broadstone

Why?

I stand there still,
Lonely in the playground,
Watching all the others have fun in their games,
Should I say something?
Would they laugh?
And shout and call me names?
Bullied.

Why?
Out of every boy and girl,
Why me?

They sneer at me,
I wipe away the tears,
I want to join in,
I do, I do,
They say I'm too shy,
But that's just the way I am,
Bullied.

Why?
Out of every boy and girl,
Why me?

Elisabeth Dean (12)
Broadstone Middle School, Broadstone

Through My Indian Eyes

If you look at the world through my eyes,
You will see poverty and dying across this land,
I sit and watch the world go by,
Lonely children without a home sit on the street,
They are crying for water, which they have been deprived
of for so long,
I sit and watch the world go by,
An old woman carrying a broken jar on her head,
Tries to walk where the land is cool on her poor, aching feet,
If you look at the world through my eyes,
You will see nothing but sadness floating across the
sorrow-filled land.

I sit and watch the world go by
Despair and sadness haunt my dreams,
The pictures of the white men that came and stole things
that are dear to me
I sit and watch the world go by,
My mind is filled with sadness,
All I want to do is get out,
I can't,
I sit and watch the world go by;
I pray for the *peace* and *hope,*
The new day will bring.

Katherine Brown (13)
Broadstone Middle School, Broadstone

Where Is The Honour?

Where is the ship and the captain?
Where are the brave crews winning?
They have all become robots of iron,
With no emotions showing.

Where is the cruiser and the fighters?
Where is the ion trail glowing?
They have passed into Alpha Centauri,
And they show no signs of slowing.

Where is the frigate and the gunner?
Where is the torpedo homing?
They have been replaced by metal,
Silicone chips growing.

Where is the risk and excitement?
Where is the adrenaline flowing?
They have all passed into the shadow,
Because of gleaming men ruling.

Where is the honour and the valour?
Where are the bright medals gleaming?
They have vanished along with their owners,
Into the dark world beyond knowledge.

Adam Refoy (12)
Broadstone Middle School, Broadstone

Life

What is life?
What is life for?
What are the answers to these questions?
Can they be answered?
All these questions rush into my head at the speed of light.

I walk around the back streets of London.
On the floor lies a man with soggy clothes and a blanket,
What has he done to deserve this?
As I walk further, the streets get dark like Hell.
Maybe the man did deserve to live life on the wet streets.

I get to the end of the back streets.
I look around, everyone is happy, as if they are in Heaven.

What is life?
What is life for?
What are the answers to these questions?
Can they be answered?
All these questions rush into my head at the speed of light
What are the answers?

Brett Champion (12)
Broadstone Middle School, Broadstone

Alone At Sea

I was all alone, the boat rocked gently,
Side to side, back and forth,
Swish, swish, swish went the waves as they
Lapped against the side of the boat.

I was all alone, there was a slight breeze,
Whoosh, there was a sudden blow of wind,
Whoosh, whoosh, whoosh went the wind as the gentle breeze
Turned into a brewing storm.

I was all alone, the storm became violent,
Smash! The boat cracked,
Bang, flash, bang went the thunder and lightning
As the boat got torn apart.

I was all alone, the boat started to sink,
Creak, the boat shuddered,
Groan, creak, groan went the boat as it started to sink,
And it took me with it.
All alone.

Ben Miles (13)
Broadstone Middle School, Broadstone

Down, Down

Down, down deep in the sea
The man lies all alone,
The sea nymphs swim around, around
As he lies slowly drifting away.

Down, down deep in the sea
The man lies all alone,
Among the small and colourful fish
Just lying there, waiting.

Down, down deep in the sea
The man lies all alone,
Constantly battered by the current
Hoping that his day will come.

Down, down deep in the sea
The man lies all alone,
Beside him crabs scuttle by
Wishing, hoping he'll soon be free.

Emma Cran (13)
Broadstone Middle School, Broadstone

Once I Was Born

Once I was born,
At All Saints Hospital.
I could hear many different sounds,
But these meant nothing.
There I lay, in my mother's arms,
My father hovering over me.
How proud the grin upon his face,
And the smile that my mother gave.
They watched me sleep,
And I drifted off and began to dream.

Frances Sales (11)
Chatham Grammar School for Girls, Chatham

Delicate Babies

Babies are born, all soft and sweet,
Delicate fingers, hands and feet.
They can cry and whine, day and night
But soon stop, when you cuddle them tight.

Babies have that 'baby' smell,
They are very clean (you can tell!)
Put them on the floor and in no time at all,
They will be crawling their very first crawl.

Cute and cuddly, playing with toys,
So cute little girls and cute little boys,
They are so cute, but can be naughty,
And at food time, they can be naughty.

And alas, soon it is bedtime
Mummies singing a soft little rhyme,
Babies all so soft, asleep,
And mothers keep having a quick little peep.

Bethany Eves (12)
Chatham Grammar School for Girls, Chatham

I Am Born

I lie in my big warm cot,
So quietly, so quietly.
My mother comes in the room,
So quietly, so quietly.
She touches my soft head,
So softly, so softly.
My head is as soft as a baby's cheek,
Very soft, very soft!
My mum picks me up so she can
Cuddle me, cuddle me.
I cry as she
Wakes me up, wakes me up.
So I can snuggle up to have my warm milk!

Sarah Mace (12)
Chatham Grammar School for Girls, Chatham

He Took Everything From Me!

I was the favourite until 'he' came along,
I was the favourite then it all went wrong,
He cries and he whines, until he gets his way,
That was my line; he's in 'my face!'

He steals my toys and he steals my mummy,
He even stole my little dummy!
I feel this way, though, I can't deny,
All I wanna do is cry,
'it looks like it's his bedtime!'

'Hooray, I get my mummy back,'
Let's put away his small train track,
'Yawn,' it looks like my time too.
'Goodnight!'

Yasmin Gayle (12)
Chatham Grammar School for Girls, Chatham

I Am Born

As my mum rushed into hospital
I rushed out
Home, and my sister and brother annoyed me.
My sister put bubbles in my face,
My brother stroked my soft cheeks,
I was known as 'soft Father Christmas!'
I did not cry much
So my mum was glad!
I sat on grandad's lap,
I was scared about if I would fall off,
Until much later, when I fell,
Off my tricycle,
Where I cried like mad!
Blood trickled down my face,
Like at a race
That was when I cried like mad!

Helen Coote (12)
Chatham Grammar School for Girls, Chatham

Signing Up In Vain!

Back from the line,
We trudge in vain,
While the shells whistle and whine,
Soon we'll be back there again.

Lice! Lice! Burn them away!
Scrabbling for the lighter,
While we burn we pray,
We collapse in exhaustion, everything quieter.

Someone shakes out their cold, wet boot,
Something comes tumbling out – part of their *foot!*
We then weep as loud as rain,
Pelting on a windowpane.

The thought of fighting fills our heads,
To load our guns and head back to war,
It's a thought all of us dreads,
To fight again and rest no more.

My nightmare full of rats and rain,
Boys being fools, signing up in vain.

Rebecca Payne (13)
Chatham Grammar School for Girls, Chatham

When I Was Born

When I was born,
I was wrapped up tight
In a blanket, warm and white
I began to cry,
But I did not know why
I was then surrounded,
By curious faces
I didn't seem to have much space.

Amy McElwaine (11)
Chatham Grammar School for Girls, Chatham

I Am Born

I feel the soft touch of my mum's chest,
She's rubbing my soft bald head,
She's thinking, *how small my darling baby is,*
She hands me over to my dad,
My dad holds me tight,
Showing me to my family, feeling proud,
My uncle calls me Kimberly,
The next day they let me go home,
My dad goes to work; me and mum are left alone,
She sings me a lullaby and I nod off,
My mum can smell my baby scent,
My mum is left in peace,
She goes to sleep while she can,
Without worrying about me, 'Zzzzz.'

Kimberly Hoather (11)
Chatham Grammar School for Girls, Chatham

I Am Born

Baby
I'm cradled in a pair of arms,
Not to be disturbed,
I see a pair of loving eyes,
And I know I'm home,
I hug her tight,
Never wanting to let go,
I fall into a deep sleep.

Mum
I look down and see,
A pair of tiny arms and feet,
And small brown eyes,
Wide open staring back at me,
Slowly,
Slowly she falls to sleep.

Sophie Byrne (11)
Chatham Grammar School for Girls, Chatham

I Am Born

When I was born I was one week late,
But it wasn't that long to wait,
As sweet as a newborn lamb they say,
Cute and healthy, born in May,
I looked pretty in pink in my frilly dresses,
With ribbons in my curly blonde tresses,
Big blue eyes and skin so fair,
Cuddling my favourite teddy bear,
I laughed and gurgled, cried and slurped,
Screamed and dribbled, smiled and burped,
I yelled and shrieked, chuckled and bawled,
Kicked my legs and finally crawled,
My mum and dad were so proud of me,
Their beautiful, bouncing, bonny baby.

Stephanie Powell (11)
Chatham Grammar School for Girls, Chatham

I Love Boys

I love boys they are the best
But sometimes they must give it a rest
Kenzie is the one for me
The age difference doesn't bother me.

I love Blazin' Squad too
They're much better than Blue
They can't sing at all
But I wouldn't mind giving them a call.

I have lots of boy mates
And we always go out on dates
I love boys all together
I will now and forever.

Connie Rogers (13)
Chatham Grammar School for Girls, Chatham

Christmas

People love this time of year,
Some celebrate by drinking champagne and beer,
Some have great and all night parties
Whilst children have presents and sweets such as Smarties.

A lot of people believe that Christmas was made by Jesus
Who was sent by God
Jesus was the one that fed five thousand with bread and cod.
He was born on the 25th of December
Christmas Day makes this easier to remember.

Christmas Day is real when it starts to snow,
This then makes you know
You will be outside all day
Going down hills in a sleigh.

Christmas is a time for having fun
You even enjoy it with no sun
People on the special day watch TV
But the programmes on are very cheesy!

Naomi Bathgate (13)
Chatham Grammar School for Girls, Chatham

Red Nose Day

Raise money for charity
Buy a red nose
Think of all the people
And where your money goes

Raise money for charity
You don't need much to impress
Every little helps
Because in Africa there is less

Raise money for charity
Buy a red nose
Think of all the people
And where your money goes.

Marie Hart (13)
Chatham Grammar School for Girls, Chatham

Wendy West

Wendy West from Washington,
Was a complex girl, you know,
She controlled the animals and plants,
Plus birds and food and snow.

Mysterious as this may seem,
There's more than meets the eye,
No ordinary hypnotist,
But cunning, also sly.

Look into the indigo eyes,
And hear a voice that drips,
With superior perfection,
And not one single slip.

So do come forth and see her,
Even though she's only small
For Wendy West from Washington,
Is a hypnotist and knows all.

Stephanie Broodbank (12)
Chatham Grammar School for Girls, Chatham

The Views Of A War

When will this war cease?
When will this war end?
So many dying,
My brother, our father, a friend.

'I'm fine, I'm doing well,
We've spent loads of time in a trench.
So after all the mud, and all the sweat,
We've created a terrible stench.'

'Come on, work harder,
Do you want to lose your head?
We're not stopping,
Until all those Germans are dead.'

Alex Cachia (12)
Chatham Grammar School for Girls, Chatham

To Die In The Trenches

Trudging through the trenches in the night,
Awake, yet sleeping, on sentry duty in fright.
The vile air reminding me of coagulated blood,
Our hands all torn, bleeding, and covered by mud.

Rats! Rats! We must kill them quick!
Their fur - greasy, brown and hardly thick.
We see them skitting across the floor,
Rushing through our trenches to our dugout's door.

My friends and family are all said to be missing,
The bombs come down, whining and hissing.
In dreams all night, still, I am bleeding,
The Germans always growing and constantly breeding.

The face of an old friend I recognise,
Lying in a trench with mud as his disguise,
His body lays limp and his face all but bone,
I fear for my own life, and for those back at home.

The guns are always thundering in the distance,
The bodies are thrown away with such insistence,
I hate those men back in England with their glory,
Who say, *'Dulce et Decorum est, pro patria mori.'*

Jessica Pocock (13)
Chatham Grammar School for Girls, Chatham

Jealousy

What is jealousy?
Jealousy is the black thundery feeling
Buried deep inside everyone.
It pops up occasionally and goes back down
It never runs out
Jealousy thrives on the thought of being seen.
It's always ready to show itself
To make you look bad.

Lucy Essenhigh (13)
Chatham Grammar School for Girls, Chatham

Waiting

In the trench I sit and wait,
For that dreaded whistle that I hate,
I lay awake, wishing for food,
I'm in a very bad mood.

There's the whistle that I hate,
I wonder why I don't run to the gate.
I go over the top, fire my gun,
The German soldiers turn and run!

Why, oh why, did I sign up for the war?
Why, oh why, I'm very poor,
This ain't a lot of fun,
I'm surprised I'm not on the run.

In the trench, I sit and wait,
For once again . . .
That dreaded whistle that I hate.

Victoria Gibbs (12)
Chatham Grammar School for Girls, Chatham

I Am Born

Hush, come close, restless one
I will hold you my baby,
I will sing you a lullaby,
I will smother you so sweetly!
It is time to close your eyes,
Droop your head,
And drift off to the land of nod.
I feel your skin, so soft and gentle,
Comforting me, easing my pain.
I love you so dearly,
And I will never leave your side,
For I am your mother,
And you are my pride.

Toni Paterson (12)
Chatham Grammar School for Girls, Chatham

The Cruel War

There are a lot of men dead around me,
Some of them I knew.
Many of the sights, I do not want to see,
And I knew, that with every breath I drew,
Another life would fall.
Guns are continually firing,
While I am standing by the wall,
A bullet just missed me but we never stop trying.

Will the rain ever stop falling?
The trenches flow with mud, trench foot is everywhere.
With high-pitched squeals the rats are calling,
They swim past the bodies that lie there.
The call rings out, *'Gas! Gas!'*
Masks at the ready, we wait in fear.
A cold and confused mass,
In spite of it all, few shed a tear.

I am next to go into no-man's-land,
Listening for those fearful words.
'Over the top,' comes the command,
With an almighty heave, I clamber forward.
At first I thought it was good to fight,
To help my king and country win,
Right now I see no light,
What an awful mess we're in . . .

Hannah Starr (13)
Chatham Grammar School for Girls, Chatham

I'm Not Coming Home

The sun rises ahead of us,
Marching to the east.
It glares at us, uninviting to us,
Like a jail cell of blood in the sky.

The stars are crying out,
Weeping, as none will return.
Then we hear the deafening shout . . .
Of guns that will haunt my dreams forever.

The bombs sing to us a long goodnight,
Falling, aiming for us,
In the middle of this fight,
That cannot be won, only lost.

We pay the cost,
As the cry goes up,
We all run, now we are all lost,
Asleep, never to wake.

I can see my comrades around me,
Dying, sinking into their end . . .
Then I realise they are with me,
I am with them and I'm not coming home.

Rebecca Birch (13)
Chatham Grammar School for Girls, Chatham

The Battlefield

The men all hurry to load their guns,
Already tired, already scared,
By merciful death and the everlasting sun,
And the bodies, blown apart on the battlefield.

The damaged soldiers go over the edge,
One by one, charging forwards,
They close their eyes, block all their senses,
And dream of life back home.

The pungent smell of burning flesh,
And the dismembered bodies that lie fresh in the black mud,
Trampled by the tread of ongoing soldiers,
Accepting that soon their life will be over.

The shells fly over like swooping birds,
And the machine guns start to fire.
One by one, the soldiers plunge into the mire,
Where they will eternally rest, lost, on the battlefield.

Stephanie Cornwell (12)
Chatham Grammar School for Girls, Chatham

I Am Born

When I was born,
I was right on time.
My mum said she had shivers,
Down her spine
Everybody's attention was on me,
That's the way I liked it.
Everybody could see.
My brother would never leave me alone,
I would scream with a high-pitched tone.
It was all too much,
I would fall asleep
With one single touch.

Nicola Dobinson (12)
Chatham Grammar School for Girls, Chatham

World War I Poem

Bang! Thick yellow clouds everywhere,
Quick! I'm blinded, where's my mask?
Mustard gas now fills the air,
'What next Sarge?' We all ask . . .

'Keep focussed men, and don't lose your head,'
Bangs and blasts, and dirt and mud.
'Just keep going or else you're dead.'
God help us all and save our blood.

Must keep going, don't stand still,
Charlie's fallen, he's my mate.
Not much further to that next hill,
Goodbye Charlie, it's too late.

At long last we are back at base,
Hundreds wounded can barely walk.
Battered and bruised and cuts on their faces,
Solemn soldiers, no one can talk.

Rosemary Brennan (12)
Chatham Grammar School for Girls, Chatham

She Is Born

Lying in her soft white cot,
Smiling her sweet, sweet smile.
Will she cry or not?
She's drifting off on a cloud,
I'm watching her fly like an angel,
I'm so happy and proud.
I want her to stay small,
I don't want her to grow up,
I don't want her to grow tall,
Will she look like me?
Or like her father?
I really can't wait to see.
What she grows up to be;
My darling daughter.

Victoria Walton (12)
Chatham Grammar School for Girls, Chatham

Think

I will tell of the disaster that happened on Boxing Day,
When everything was wiped away,
In one big wave.
Now people have no homes, food or drink,
This is the disaster that made the world think.

Family gone,
Friends gone,
Nearly everything, gone in just a few blinks,
This is the disaster that made the world think.

Whilst everyone here was partying away,
The people in Thailand were left in dismay.
When we heard the news there were no more glasses clinking.
But everyone sat down, deeply thinking.

Money pots and appeals,
Now these people can eat a meal,
Everyone is pleased that they can be helped,
Just remember, this really was a disaster that made the world think.

Paige Gibson (13)
Chatham Grammar School for Girls, Chatham

The Woods

The mysterious woods
All dark and black
Always looking behind my back.
The owls fly and so do bats
Their eyes pierce through the cracks
The wolves howl and hunt
The leader walks at the front
The night goes on and you can only wonder,
What happens in the woods, the place down under
A crack, a howl and a rustle in the night
Nothing can give you more of a fright
You're on your own in the dangerous woods
The frights, the wariness, run away, I would!

Stephanie Coney (12)
Chatham Grammar School for Girls, Chatham

I Am Born

Here I am!
My life - newly born.
I watch my parents gazing down,
They are too delighted to become forlorn,
My eyes that droop,
My widening mouth,
I overturn in my cradle,
I face the south.
I awake to strange burbles,
My ears hear the noise,
There is a pain in my stomach,
Now I make the noise.
So into my mouth a bottle is popped.
And I suckle upon it . . .
Now the noises have stopped.

Sarah Andrew (12)
Chatham Grammar School for Girls, Chatham

Sleeping Sweetly

The baby sleeps,
Sleeping so sweetly.
And the room is silent . . .
I see her clearly.
But all I hear is her breathing softly,
She's like an angel floating in the clouds,
Like a beautiful golden eagle gliding across the sunset.
Its wings are outstretched,
I see her yawn . . .
I hear her wail.
Her arms call out to me,
I hold her close.
And the crying seems to fade . . .
. . . away . . .

Amy Le Conte (12)
Chatham Grammar School for Girls, Chatham

A Dream That Takes You To A World Of Your Own

I lie down in my cot,
Sleepy as a sloth,
As my mum,
Comes in my bedroom,
And turns off the light.
In my sleep,
I have a dream,
A dream where,
I am floating high.
I see my mum,
Right by my side.
She will always . . .
Be nearby.
Then I see my,
Chestnut horse,
He's giving me rides,
Through the forest.
Now this is where,
I end my dream,
With love and care,
All around me.
I'll stop it now,
So it will stay the same.
And when it's gone,
I'll dream it again.

Megan Davis (11)
Chatham Grammar School for Girls, Chatham

Bumpy Ride!

A poem is a bumpy ride,
It takes you through life,
It takes you through the seas and mountains,
To anywhere you want.

A poem is a bumpy ride.
It takes you to the end,
It takes you round the bushes,
Lets your imagination run wild.

A poem is a bumpy ride.
It takes you through the forest,
Through thick and thin,
But don't worry, you'll soon see . . .

Follow it, and believe in yourself.
Trust it will guide you around,
The beginning and the end.
You'll just be doing the right thing.

You'll be back where you started,
For when you look at it,
You'll see that's what life really is.
'C'est la vie!'

Adekunbi Okufi (13)
Chatham Grammar School for Girls, Chatham

Dying For Your Country

Backs aching, trudging through mud,
Moaning and groaning about our wet feet,
The trenches look like a flood.
Nothing will alarm us, we will not retreat.
Some people are lying on the floor with fright.
We are near our trench.
Darkness is all around, it must be nearly night.

What if the gas comes and fills my face?
Where is my mask?
Is it in its case?
If the gas does flow,
I won't be able to put my gas mask on,
I will not be able to run.
I guess I'll just die with the rest of them, gone!

Attack! The enemy is about to attack,
My friend has been shot in the leg and arm,
He falls in front of me,
To my obvious alarm.
His face crumples in pain, like the limbs of an old oak tree.

I see him every night in my dreams.
Can you think of that dream?

I pick him up and put him over my shoulder,
Only in your worst nightmares can you see what I've seen.
The air is getting colder.
Blood is pouring from his wounds, far from clean.
Every step I take he shouts in pain,
Clutching, gripping and squeezing his arm.
His hanging limbs like a broken branch under strain.
No one is very calm
The old lie told over and over again:
Dying for your country surely can't hurt.

Sarah Burley (13)
Chatham Grammar School for Girls, Chatham

Believe What You Want . . .

(Inspired by 'Dulce et Decorum est' by Wilfred Owen)

All the men and women say it's your duty,
'Dulce et Decorum est . . .'
All the girls say, 'You're a cutie,'
But beware of what they tell you.
Don't believe everything they say,
Because everything about war is drenched in blood.
Trust me, I've been there, it's not a pretty sight,
The blood, terror, will haunt you all night.

'Run! Run!' The Germans are coming - 'Boy don't dawdle!'
Load guns . . . Fix bayonets . . . 'Come on lad!'
But someone is still trying, crying as it were,
He had such a struggle, but we could not help.
So before you come and try to be brave, remember this lie;
'Dulce et Decorum est.'

As we stood there, waiting for them to come,
Something was in my mind.
This is the part which decides if I live or die . . .

If in my mind comes a pleasant thought,
It disappears straight away.
Because I think of the moment in war, when we all fought,
The pain. The blood. The death.
Like a man in pain of misery.
As I see a man die at my feet, I think,
Why am I here? Killing an innocent man.
Is this what love for my country . . .
Has to return?
So my friends, believe what you want . . .
But how dare you say,
'Dulce et Decorum est.'

Scarlett Shade (13)
Chatham Grammar School for Girls, Chatham

Cruentus Verum (The Bloody Reality)

A shell screams ahead
And all through the base
Not a heartbeat was silent
Not a smile on one face.

They come into war
With love in their hearts
With hope in their eyes
But that hope's blow apart.

They cling to each other like mother and child
The heart-stopping cries echo as they bolt through the wild.

There, many sit, in water and mud
And wipe the dried and caking blood.

They send their last prayers up to the sky
With no more tears left to cry.

Some sit in trenches, the terrified men
While they shoot at others, petrified like them.

You see the bodies pile on the floor
It's the beginning of the end, the First World War.

Their hearts now shattered, their feet are numb
They now understand the *Cruentus Verum.*

Amy Russell (13)
Chatham Grammar School for Girls, Chatham

Life At War

Lying down in a damp, cold trench,
Rain hitting me; I am drenched.
A flare goes up, into the night,
Here comes the gunshots, it seems so bright.

'Guns at the ready lads,' I hear the sergeant cry,
Here comes the Germans, one looks me in the eye.
I shoot at him, I miss, I'm glad,
He's too young to be here, he's only a lad.

I think of home, I see my mother,
She's in the larder, holding my brother.
My eyes well up, I start to cry,
But I carry on shooting, with my head held high.

The gunshots die down the night is quiet,
So different from the no-man's-land riot.
I notice I have a hole in my leg,
I cry out for help, but the others are dead.

I see someone running, into the night,
It's my father, but wait, he died last night.
I close my eyes, I shake my head,
I realise then that I am dead.

So you folks out there, that urge boys to go to war,
You wouldn't dare if you saw what I saw.

Lucy Riley (12)
Chatham Grammar School for Girls, Chatham

Scared Of Life Itself

This young boy,
He sits in his room trying not to think
Of the terrible day he has had,
But he has flashbacks in his dreams,
Waking up sweating and petrified of tomorrow.

This young boy,
He never goes out, he is too scared of the abuse he will receive,
He is bruised on the outside but even more on the inside.
He has a broken heart where he has been hurt so many times.
He has no friends and no one to talk to.
Every day is a huge threat for him.
And the word school makes him cry.

This young boy,
Is scared of life itself.

Carla Esposito (12)
Chatham Grammar School for Girls, Chatham

I Am Born

Tiny hands and feet,
I watch as she falls asleep,
The night draws near,
I see visions so clear,
Of her being so deeply loved,
Hearts jump out,
I hear them shout,
As two white doves,
Show the love.
I hold her tight,
So close to me all night,
I don't want her to grow,
I just want to show,
I'll be there all the way.

Lauren Clarke (12)
Chatham Grammar School for Girls, Chatham

Easter Time

E aster is a time
A bout sharing and caring with
S omething like chocolate
T o give as a gift
E veryone is smiling and
R olling with laughter.

T o see the big cake
I , the flour did sift
M um's in the kitchen
E xacting the dinner.

A fter a time
T ogether we eat.

H appy and joking
O ver who ends up choking
M egumi has helped
E veryone cuts their meat.

Emily Davie (12)
Chatham Grammar School for Girls, Chatham

Forgiveness - Haikus

Something special is
The gift of forgiveness so
Hey! Don't just waste it.

Sometimes people don't
Understand how it feels to
Be pushed out the way.

But forgiveness is
A tool you can use to help
Just like love is too!

Krysia Waldock (13)
Chatham Grammar School for Girls, Chatham

Do You Know?

Do you know what goes on every day?
Well for the third world countries it's awful.
Day and night full of pain and hunger,
You really wouldn't believe what they go through.

Every day the daughters go out,
Collecting dirty water to drink,
They get so many diseases just from the water,
No wonder thousands die every year.

But help is at hand from celebs at the 'mo',
Comic Relief raising money from them all
Helping to give them fresh water and food
Giving them an education and tools and many more.

This makes such a difference to people in need,
It puts such a smile on their face
Diseases are fewer and so are the deaths,
People helping each other just for the best.

So would you give just a little each month?
To help these poor innocent people that suffer.
Many are still in need of help,
While you sit back,
Taking for granted what you have.

Rachel Newberry (12)
Chatham Grammar School for Girls, Chatham

The Puppet Makers

Made for nothing,
Used for nothing,
Alone in all my ways,
Lonely, lost and heartless,
The puppet makers say.
When they pull, I move,
When they shout, I cry,
When they hurt, I hurt more,
It's misty all around me,
It's hard to see things near,
But the puppet makers say,
That they can make things clear,
I walk as a shiver,
I shiver as a walk,
But when they're around me,
I can't even talk.
The words they once said,
Were starting to make sense,
I didn't seem to mind
Them becoming like my fence.
They came closer and closer,
But then I once said
'Leave me alone!'
And then I was dead!

Celene Tighe (12)
Chatham Grammar School for Girls, Chatham

A Poem On My Family

My family can be festive,
All families can be fun,
I wonder what my family is like?
Shall I tell you about my one?

I'll start off with my mum,
Who works hard every day
Keeps up happy and behaved
And then she gets her pay.

Paying the bills is over,
Now she can have some fun
After school on Friday
With friends that don't weigh a ton.

Last thing about my mum
She loves me loads
After having three kids
There are never any lows.

Now it's the turn of my dad,
Who absolutely loves his sport,
Badminton is the one,
That he has always sought.

Also, he loves Manchester United,
They're his favourite team,
After all, they lost their self-esteem.

Oh, and one last point,
Game, set and match,
Maybe other people can help,
Then they'll always make the catch!

So, and one last note,
Most of my family is in this poem,
So tell me about your family,
That they are the best!

Stephanie Alexander (13)
Chatham Grammar School for Girls, Chatham

Red Nose Poem

Oh how I love being silly,
    On Red Nose Day,
It's so very funny,
    On Red Nose Day.

    But . . .

It's not just about that,
    On Red Nose Day,
It's about helping people,
    On Red Nose Day.

All you have to do is
    Give a little money,
It would go so very far.

If everyone did it,
    Then no one would be poor,
They would live like us,
    And shop in the local store.

It's about rich countries,
    Stretching out their hand,
And helping countries,
    That need this helping hand.

I wish that Red Nose Day,
    Was not every other year,
But just because it is,
    Have no fear.

Help everyday,
    It's just as fun,
And you'll have a happy feeling,
    Knowing you've helped someone.

Bryony Howard (12)
Chatham Grammar School for Girls, Chatham

Clubbin'

It's time to party, I'm ready to impress
I hear the pulsing music booming away
I'm boogying in my sexy red dress
Tonight I'm outrageous and I've come out to play

My killer-heeled stilettos are forgotten
Four hours non-stop dancing, 'cause life's too short
I see you looking, your cheeks start to hotten
I focus on the music, no time for thoughts.

I shimmy to the rhythm across the floor
My feet go crazy to the wild dance beats
When it's over you'll have to drag me to the door
So much dancing, no one's using the seats.

I feel so free as my body floats away
Dancing forever, never stop clubbin', my life,
Dancing forever, never stop clubbin', my life,
Dancing forever, never stop clubbin', my life.

Abisola Omotayo (13)
Chatham Grammar School for Girls, Chatham

My Mum

My mum's name is Mandy,
She's always very handy.
Whenever I fall and hurt my knee,
My mum is always there for me.

My mum smells like a bunch of flowers,
It's like she has got magical powers.
My mum has got eyes in the back of her head,
But that's what she's always said.

I love my mum and she loves me.
And that's what makes us such a happy family.

Samantha Harries (12)
Chatham Grammar School for Girls, Chatham

Heartbroken

She was such a lovely lady,
Everyone loved her,
Including me,
But now I'm heartbroken.

She always used to sing merrily,
But now she cries,
Of the confusion of what's going on in her mind,
And now she's heartbroken.

This evil spirit is taking her over,
Now she's trapped in a different world,
This spirit is called Alzheimer's
And everyone is heartbroken.

Now she has gone forever,
She won't remember me again,
I haven't got a grandma anymore,
And that's why we're heartbroken.

Lisa Boland (13)
Chatham Grammar School for Girls, Chatham

Jungle

Creepy crawlies, slimy snakes
Sliver through the swamps and lakes,
Leaves rustle, you hear a growl
There's a lion waiting on the prowl.

Do look out for what lies ahead,
Do not get yourself misled.
The jungle's a pretty scary place,
Don't stand in an open space.

Never go through a jungle alone,
Especially if you're accident-prone
Be aware, look out where you tread,
Otherwise you may end up dead!

Katie Bottle (13)
Chatham Grammar School for Girls, Chatham

They Can't Scare Me!

If you come to our house in the middle of the night,
You're sure to get an awful fright.
It's choc-a-bloc full of ghosts, you see,
But whatever they do they can't scare me!

There are two little baby ghosts playing on the stairs,
And a headless horseman saying his prayers
A spook in the toilet having a pee,
But whatever they do they can't scare me!

There's a ghost in the garden, playing with the cat,
And another on the patio, wearing granny's hat;
Apparitions in the kitchen having their tea,
But whatever they do they can't scare me!

There's a boggart in the chimney slowing up the fire,
And a cellar-full of spirits, all singing in a choir.
There are zombies in the parlour, watching TV,
But whatever they do, they can't scare me!

If you come to our house in the middle of the night,
You're sure to get an awful fright,
It's choc-a-bloc full of ghosts, you see,
But . . . whatever . . . they . . . do . . .
But whatever they . . .
But what . . .
But . . . !
Aaarrrggghhh!

Stacey Bertolla (13)
Chatham Grammar School for Girls, Chatham

Prisoner

He lies in the cell wishing it were over,
Wishes he is drunk, although he is sober.
Wants to forget what has happened in his life,
His daughter has left him and so has his wife.
Ten more days must he face alone,
No one to hear him shout or moan.

He wishes he had at least one friend,
Someone on whom he can trust and depend.
He dreams of the days he was happy and free,
The last time he saw a train or a tree.

Three more days must he face alone,
No one to hear him shout or moan.
He cannot wait to be free,
Away from this captivity.
Now when he thinks about the world going by,
He knows that the end of his prison sentence is nigh.

No more days must he face alone,
There is now someone there to hear him shout and moan.
He now lives his life being happy and free,
He now has seen a train and a tree.
He now has a chance to make new friends,
People on whom he can trust and depend.

Ellen Jones (13)
Chatham Grammar School for Girls, Chatham

She . . .

She cried out her eyes
At school every day
Never a day of peace for her,
But they always say
She is not to tell.

She sits on her own
Knowing they will come
They rob her of everything
But she never tells anyone,
She is too scared.

She is suffering quietly
So I must help
I told all who listened
Everything there was to tell
They did all they could.

She doesn't cry anymore
She isn't robbed like before
The bullies have been sent away
Today she lives for a lot more
Not afraid of anything.

Tulsi Patel (12)
Chatham Grammar School for Girls, Chatham

Winter

The harsh winter day was beginning to dawn,
People were waking to a snowy morn.
The freezing icicles clinging to trees,
A little red robin flying in the frosty breeze.
The snowy rooftops all white and shiny,
The snowflakes falling were ever so tiny,
The moon was rising through the crisp winter sky,
Another winter's day was beginning to die.

Shannon Bennett (12)
Chatham Grammar School for Girls, Chatham

War, War, War!

War, war, war is a country for many lives,
It is to fight with many knives.
It is too much hate,
It is to die instead of fate.

War, war, war is a big deal,
It isn't how we feel.
It is very, very sad,
To lose your loved ones like your dad.

War, war, war defeating with all their might,
When all they do is fight.
With mud up to their knees,
When covered in fleas.

War, war, war goes bang, bang, bang,
And kills all their gang.
It is now time to fly,
Up to the heavens and die.

Danielle-Leigh Nolan (12)
Chatham Grammar School for Girls, Chatham

Night-Time

The sky is like a black velvet cloak
Studded with jewels.
At night-time, all nocturnal creatures rule.
Owls seek,
Children sleep,
Badgers blunder,
OAPs slumber,
Bats flap,
Pets nap,
Humans doze,
As doors close.
Nocturnal animals rule till dawn
When humans rise in the morn.

Beth Champ (12)
Chatham Grammar School for Girls, Chatham

The Day I Turned Into A Dolphin

A beautiful summer's day . . .
Not too long ago.
I was with Mum and Dad on holiday,
The day was going slow.
Seconds slipping by like snails,
Each minute felt like ten.
I couldn't wait until I could . . .
Go swimming once again.

You see, I'm fond of swimming.
Can do breast stroke and float.
I can never wait until Dad says,
'Let's go, now get your coat.'
How the hell was I to know?
Something strange would be,
For this day felt like normal,
But I began to feel queasy.

So I dived into the cool, blue lake,
Which was sparkling in the sun.
Strangely, I could swim better,
I had so much fun.
But when it was time to dry myself,
I found that I had changed . . .

Instead of hands I now had flippers,
My skin turned bluey-grey.
My dad saw, and looked amazed,
'My dear, oh dear!' I heard him say.
For I was no longer me,
I had turned into a dolphin - whoopee!

Now my family visit me everyday,
In my little lake, forever will I play.

Lauren O'Brien (13)
Chatham Grammar School for Girls, Chatham

Poverty's Prayer

Dear God,

In the morning let there be rain
Let my children run and play in it
Let them live to dance and sing
Please Lord, let there be rain.

Let me survive long enough to see them grow
Please let them grow always
To live a long and fruitful time
Oh Lord may I survive.

Let there be life in my tribe
Don't make me lose again
Spare my children all the heartache
Oh Lord let there be life.

Let water run so close to us
That we could wash every day
Let my daughter rest her feet
Oh Lord please let it run.

Pleas God spare my children
The pain within, the pain that racks my heart
Let them live to have joyousness
Oh Lord spare them the aches inside.

We work so hard
Our children starve
My daughter's feet are bruised
I am starting to wonder . . .

Are you even listening?

Courtney Overton-Edwards (13)
Chatham Grammar School for Girls, Chatham

The Rain Comes Down

The rain comes down once again,
As I trudge my way through the thick sludge,
We just lost a few in a surprise attack.

The rain comes down once again.
As the sickly sweet stench of rotting flesh surrounds me,
Mutilated remains sleep, never to wake again.

The rain comes down once again,
As I become adrift in a sea of the dead,
Old friends now with sunken faces and strange, rolling eyes.

This war is a waste,
The waste of time,
The waste of lives,
All the waste . . .

Another gas attack.
I struggle with my gas mask but I can't get it on,
Too late,
I breathe, I fall,
As the rain comes down once again.

Bernie Doyle (12)
Chatham Grammar School for Girls, Chatham

Snow

I watch the snow tumbling softly out of the sky,
It fills me with great sadness as it makes me wonder why,
Why can't we have snow more than three times a year?
But the answer is sinister, something everyone should fear -
Global warming, and its presence here with us.
But politicians are useless, there's no time to discuss,
We need to right our wrongs, to stop relying on our cars.
Or Earth could go the same way as Venus or as Mars!
Both options are fatal; we must do something now,
Everyone must help, there's no question of who or how!
It's not 'The Day After Tomorrow,' it's happening today.
That's why we must stop carbon emissions, in every possible way!

Anya Gelman (13)
Chatham Grammar School for Girls, Chatham

I Am Homeless . . . Are You Surprised!

I am homeless; I live on the streets,
Sleeping in a doorway, the cold seeps through my clothes.
I wear dirty clothes and have nothing to eat,
Will somebody help me, who knows?

Travelling the streets all day long,
Longing for food and somewhere to stay.
I have to keep on travelling and be strong,
Will somebody help me, who knows?

Everyday I dream, dream, dream,
I wish for a home and food.
I hope one day to have a bath and be clean,
Will somebody help me, who knows?

I would love to have someone to care for me,
To have love and care that someone shows.
Everyday the dirty streets are all I see,
How did I end up like this?
Who knows?

Chloe Parsons (13)
Chatham Grammar School for Girls, Chatham

A New Arrival

There's a new arrival in the field,
Its mother guards it like a shield.
Its eyes so deep, brown and small,
It can hardly stand, not at all.

As it finally finds its feet,
We give it something to eat.
We stroke its face of soft chestnut coat,
It's swaying on its feet like a wave under a boat.

The wet black nose appears over the gate,
It still looks scared: an expected state,
People stop to look, can't help but stare,
At the gorgeous foal, so weak and fair.

Grace Kemp (13)
Chatham Grammar School for Girls, Chatham

The Tsunami Disaster

As the tsunami struck and shook,
The Indian Ocean,
Asia was left in ruins . . .

As Boxing Day approached,
People prayed,
Prayed for their lives.

This is what it took for us to see,
Not everyone is as fortunate as we,
Disaster struck,
That was the end.

Nurses tended,
To the wounded,
But still many people,
Never returned.

People giving,
Charities collecting,
But nothing . . .

Not even money,
Could save the lives,
Of the people that died.

Charlotte Hattley (12)
Chatham Grammar School for Girls, Chatham

Love

Love is always described,
Like a fairy tale,
Like a pretty flower,
Or a great big teddy bear.

But love is far more complex,
Not always velvet-smooth,
More like a bumpy road,
With lots of different moods.

Love can be a fairy tale,
Love can be Hell,
Love can be a beautiful sunset,
Love can be the dark night sky.

Love can be pain and deceit,
Love can be happiness and smiles,
Love can be good,
Love can be bad.

Love can be all the colours of the rainbow,
Or maybe,
Just maybe,
Love can be true.

Jessica Bunyan (13)
Chatham Grammar School for Girls, Chatham

Cheap As Lies

Blistered feet, painful like a broken heart,
Limping crooked, like an old man's teeth we trudged,
Still we continued to play our pointless part,
Even though the enemy's status had not budged.

We marched onwards, some still in their dreams of home,
Many were struggling in this nightmare of Hell,
Desperately picking out wretched lice with a comb,
I thought to myself; how much longer must we stay here and dwell?

In spite of our position the bombs continued to drop,
Dropping like violent rain to the ground,
Thinking to ourselves we would never come out on top,
Then suddenly there was no sound.

Shouts of, *'Gas! Gas! Gas!'* echoed around the trench,
Needing reflexes so quick, for strapping on my mask was a task.
Then I caught sight of someone catching the deadly stench,
That's when I realised he had no mask.

My heart sinking, I watched helpless like the dead,
Realising someone was losing their son, father or brother,
As he vomited violently I watched him with dread,
He stared at me; too horrified to look at his ghastly face, I took cover.

Yet worse was to come, we parted with his body outside,
His eyes were still boring up at us; his limbs still bleeding,
Froth still escaping his gaping mouth, making me want to hide,
Suddenly it was clear to me we were not succeeding.

Think what you want to think, do what you want to do,
But let me tell you now, I will never forget his cries,
When you sign up for war you really haven't got a clue,
Understand now, everything they tell you is as cheap as lies.

Samantha Roadnight (13)
Chatham Grammar School for Girls, Chatham

My Perfect Life

My perfect life . . . What would it be . . . ?
Of course! A world which revolved around me!
Everything I want just one call away,
I have the power to change anything, like night into day.
Then I would find a trillion pounds on the floor . . .
I would buy what I wanted, even a diamond see-saw!
Everything evil would leave us alone,
Life would be as cool as an ice cream cone!
Now for my mansion, it would reach the moon!
With a different theme for each room.
I would play all day in my giant theme park,
Dodgems! Water rides! Roller coasters in the dark!
In the background you can hear Elvis playing live in my bedroom,
Girls screaming, *oh swoon, swoon, swoon!*
Not forgetting my *gorgeous* boyfriend whom I love very much,
It's Johnny Depp! He's an angel sent from above!
Then there are my old buddies, I've known them for years,
Billion earning film stars who make me laugh and
　　　　　　　　　　　help me through my fears . . .

You may think this unrealistic . . .
You may think this untrue . . .
But hey it's my dream . . .
So what are you gonna do?

Francesca Eastwood (13)
Chatham Grammar School for Girls, Chatham

Delicate Baby

The cute baby lies in her crib, spread with baby-pink covers,
Reaching out with her tiny hands,
Making a happy noise with a smile on her face,
Snuggling up to her brand new cuddly toy,
The mother moves the innocent baby
Away from the cuddly toy to keep her from harm,
The baby strokes her mother's hand
With her soft hands and slowly falls asleep.
Silence is around; the baby lies with a soft breath,
The mother tiptoes out with a smile on her face
Watching her as she walks away,
The baby suddenly wakes,
The mother feels guilty,
She can't leave the baby,
She gently picks up the baby and takes her to the living room
Where many visitors are waiting to hold her,
The family all smile whilst looking at their new family member,
'We shall name her Scarlett,' Father announces.

Rebecca Taylor (12)
Chatham Grammar School for Girls, Chatham

My World

My world is green with a waterfall and stream
The sun lays on the rock pool with a gleam
A bird's song comes in the warm breeze that carries a flower
I feel chilled and relaxed as if I have no power
My place is quiet and safe, the only sound is the gentle trickle
This place is friendly and the bugs nearby give me a tickle
In this place I have no worries but happy thoughts and
memories sweet
And only friends and family here meet.

Sarah Mosca (13)
Chatham Grammar School for Girls, Chatham

Being Happy

I am born
My mum lying in a hospital bed
Gives a sigh of relief,
My dad, a smile on his face;
Then my mum takes me into her arms;
Her soft gentle arms, so smooth,
I begin to cry,
Not knowing why.
My dad takes me from my mum's arms,
Very gently,
And he begins to rock me;
Not hurting me, just trying to calm me down.
My mum, she is smiling at me,
Like I was making her happy!
I smile back at her
My dad laughs, so does the nurse!
Then I eventually drift off into a deep sleep.

Aarati Kapoor (12)
Chatham Grammar School for Girls, Chatham

Being Born

On the 28th of May it was hot as hot can be,
My mum sat up in a bed with my nan close beside.
Grandad rushing back, waiting for me.
Then came half-past six,
And my mum was crying out.
Quietly the small cries of me were heard.
There was happiness throughout my family.
My grandad was so proud,
Me.
A tiny baby was brought into this family.

Yasmin March (11)
Chatham Grammar School for Girls, Chatham

Admirer

My love is burning bright,
Shame it's a secret love.
My love is a shining light,
Shame it's a secret love.

When I think about her beauty,
It makes me weak.
Shame she's my secret love.
Her love for me is so, so meek,
Shame she's my secret love.

She will never be, never be mine,
Shame I'm not her secret love.
I wish we could be entwined,
Shame I'm not her secret love.

I wish I could mean so much more to her,
But I'm just her admirer.

Nancy Day (13)
Chatham Grammar School for Girls, Chatham

Furry Friend

He's nothing much but fur,
All springing and leaping,
And two round eyes of blue.

He is a staring surprise,
Light as a feather,
And as soft as a puff.

As he drops off to sleep,
With a paw on his nose,
He looks so peaceful and pure.

Kathryn Hinkley (12)
Chatham Grammar School for Girls, Chatham

Boys!

Boys just don't get feelings,
And they definitely don't understand.
They don't even know about healing,
Or want to hold your hand.

They show you off to all their friends,
They only want to use you.
They make you go round all the bends,
Oh why, oh why do boys abuse?

At times they act real keen,
But then they turn mean.
They don't show affection in public,
And they even take the mick.

I know that boys are immature,
You want to fly away like a dove,
Boys are problems for sure,
Oh why, oh why do we love . . .
. . . Boys . . .

Meghan Mudge (12)
Chatham Grammar School for Girls, Chatham

I Am Born

I see her lying still and small,
Wondering will she cry at all,
Her breathing, silent and smooth,
So peaceful, so tranquil,
The few hairs she has cling tightly to her head,
Suddenly I stand motionless, filled with dread,
Will she wake? Will she stir?
This tiny bundle fills my heart with love,
How blessed I am with this gift from above,
For evermore I will love and care for this soul,
To make her life wonderful is my only goal.

Sophie Lancaster (12)
Chatham Grammar School for Girls, Chatham

Nil Satis Nisi Optimum

These once young fighting men,
Now lie like crippled old beggars,
Haunted faces of bloody memories,
Wishing this hell they live in would end.

Rotting feet, bleeding wounds,
But still they are made to fight.
To fight for their country,
To fight for their loved ones,
To fight for justice.
So they go on fighting and starving,
Fighting for their country and loved ones and justice.

The signal is up,
Over they must go.
To look Death once more in the eyes,
For Death has nearly caught up with these men,
And so over they go.

Those wounded bodies scrambling over the wire,
They run into this land of nothing,
Then bullets rip through the air,
Catching those men off guard.

Then they fall to the ground,
Going down like flies,
Screams! Yelps!
Blistering pain spreading across the body,
There they will be left to rot,
To wither away into the ground,
Known now as men who died for their country.

Louise McEvoy (12)
Chatham Grammar School for Girls, Chatham

I Am Born

She was born,
I think she is sweet.
She cries when she's hungry or sleepy,
She screams at night when she awakes from her beautiful sleep.
You can see her heavenly dreams
Floating in a fluffy white cloud.
She wakes at sunrise screaming,
Screaming, waiting for her sour milk
I, as her mother, come and give it to her
She soon is dreaming her dreams
She sleeps sweetly
We can hear her soft snoring
I think we shall call her . . .

Rebecca Kandola.

Rebecca Kandola (11)
Chatham Grammar School for Girls, Chatham

Shall I Compare Thee To A Tin Of Beans?

(Inspired by 'Sonnet 18' by William Shakespeare)

Shall I compare thee to a tin of beans?
Hard on the outside but softer inside;
Because you look like you're more than you seem.
Damn! This is rubbish, I think I might hide.
Writing love sonnets is really quite hard.
You're so incomparable, oh why me?
I'll never make it as the next great Bard.
Why can't I do this? - I know then you'd see.
Why did I talk about a tin of beans?
Well, this poem's certainly as hard as the tin,
You are not hard but you don't seem too keen.
Oh my God, look at the mess I'm now in!
Teachers say poems need mock'ry and scorn.
Well, this one has had that all along!

Rebecca Apley (13)
Cranford House School, Wallingford

Shall I Compare Thee To The Summer's Sun?

(Inspired by 'Sonnet 18' by William Shakespeare)

Shall I compare thee to the summer's sun?
Thou art more lovely than its gleaming light.
The fright'ning darkness doth not dim your fun.
The winter dullness and the early nights
Doth not harm your fiery character.
When I am abroad thou art on my mind:
In my life thou art the highest factor.
Thou will forever be my greatest find,
But as the handsome moon falls between us,
I'm forever in the depths of despair,
Thus a comet hits me, I make no fuss.
As the blindness fades I become aware
That thou doth no longer love me at all.
You have hurt me, I shall now shrink and fall.

Hayley Jubb (12) & Michelle Sangan (13)
Cranford House School, Wallingford

You Will Always Be My Plate Of Chips

(Inspired by 'Sonnet 18' by William Shakespeare)

Shall I compare you to a plate of chips?
You are the saucy ketchup on the side.
I savour you forever on my lips,
The love I have for you I cannot hide.
Sometimes you're far too hot for me to eat,
A pinch of salt will make you more tasty.
When you are around I'm in for a treat,
But I'm warning you, my underwear's lacy!
Sometimes you're crispy, but fluffy inside,
You make me smile whenever I see you.
But soon, Amanda, you will be my bride,
Marry me, Mandy, I'll always be true.
Darling, you'll always be my plate of chips!
Oh why did you push me into that ditch?

Emma Griffin (13) & Katie Allen (12)
Cranford House School, Wallingford

A Day In The Life Of Grumpiness

Grumpiness awakes with a groan and a growl
And throws the duvet off the bed
He murmurs rude words as he stamps around
The man with pessimistic views

The house shakes when he bangs his fist
People cower when he glares at them,
With eyebrows down and shoulders hunched
The man with a scowl stuck firmly in place

A shout, a cry, a yell, a warning!
Grumpiness is coming into the town
Beware! Beware! Watch your back
He's turning round, he's going home!

As Grumpiness trudges back up the path
With a heart as hard as a dirty stone
He slams the door with a bang behind him
An old man with a key to gloom.

Lucy Goodyear (12)
Cranford House School, Wallingford

Alacrity

He dresses in his evening suit,
Ties his terrible tie in a hurry,
With a date at eight and it's only seven,
The thought of it is simply Heaven.

Come out, come out, no time to lose,
Can't drive, can't ride, only one thing left,
Put on your boots and walk, just walk,
A mile or two, one should not balk.

And soon he reaches the crystal clear lake,
The sunset water reflects his face,
Now one more face appears beside it,
Love has arrived and you cannot hide it.

Zenia Selby (10)
Cranford House School, Wallingford

Honesty

Honesty is telling the truth
No matter what the loss
No matter what the consequences
No matter what the cost.

Honesty is telling your mum
Where you really were
Where you went and what you did
And who was really there.

Honesty is giving back
The change when it's too much
Even though that crispy fiver
Was so nice to touch.

Honesty is not stealing
That watch that caught your eye
But saving all the money up
So that you can buy.

Honesty is being true
To yourself and others
Especially to your family
And most of all our mothers.

Courtenay Argyle (13)
Cranford House School, Wallingford

WHSmith

WHSmith is like an elephant standing out proud.
WHSmith's blue, the brightest colour on Earth.
WHSmith is as busy as 1,000 people trying to catch a bus.
WHSmith is a giraffe with seven different layers.
WHSmith is the best shop in the world.

Georgina Lindsey (12)
Cranford House School, Wallingford

Teenage Years

There is time in every girl's life
Where they change for the worse:
From nice, sweet kid to terrible teens
As if under a curse.

As each girl reaches the age of 13
Their interests change dramatically:
From being good, helpful and kind
To boys they turn quite rapidly.

They cover their faces with lots of make-up
And go chasing after boys,
Being grumpy, moody and stressy
They make a lot of noise.

Screaming and screeching at their parents
Is a regular scene
But all through this, their parents are needed
For comfort if people are mean.

Because although they rant and rave
They love their parents dearly:
It's not their fault that they change so much,
They are improving really!

Katherine Poulter (13)
Cranford House School, Wallingford

Confusion Haiku

A mass of merged thoughts,
Doing seven things at once,
Searching for meaning.

Jessica Leslie (14) & Katherine Sandbach (12)
Cranford House School, Wallingford

Confusion

Confusion is a man stumbling in the fog
In open country

The ground is uneven and every
Step is uncertain and frightening

Especially when the man was
Lost before the fog descended

Confusion is this man walking
Into a strange, deserted town
In the fog

In his weary haze opening
The door to a strange house

Glancing at an untouched
Hallway covered in secrets
Not seeing anything.

Charley Grimshaw (11)
Cranford House School, Wallingford

Love

Love is your first kiss in the most excellent weather
Love is two people who want always to be together
Love is the sound of a rippling waterfall
Love is the sound of the little bird's call
Love is a candlelit dinner set by a glorious beach
Love is the first bite of a juicy peach
Love is the relaxation of a spa
Love is the sight of your newly bought car
Love is red roses
Love is when your boyfriend proposes
Love is in the air
Love is everywhere!

Gemma Bridge & Rosie Jackson (11)
Cranford House School, Wallingford

What Is Love?

She guides the hands that cut the roses,
Directing the wrapping of a beautiful bouquet;
She fills the lungs of a young girl running
Along the beach on a summer's day.

She wraps you up in a blanket of warmth -
The feel of someone holding you,
She spreads her wings to soar up high,
Taking with her only those who are true.

Her river running full of emotion,
Flows down the hill with a thousand ripples,
It shimmers on an autumn's day,
Because love will always find its way.

Annabel West & Jenny Robinson (11)
Cranford House School, Wallingford

Guilt

When Guilt sees you erring,
He follows you through the town.
He taps on your shoulder,
He starts to get you down.
He's not going to go away,
Guilt's here to stay.

When Guilt sees you doing wrong,
He pulls on your sleeve.
He'll nag and get under your skin,
He's not going to leave.
Guilt will soon drive you mad!
That'll teach you for being bad!

Olivia Beazley (11)
Cranford House School, Wallingford

Fear . . .

He creeps down the gravel path,
No louder than his shadow.
Slowly . . . trembling . . .
The night a fearful sight itself,
Blacker than the crow.
Slowly . . . trembling . . .
Your heart beats harder as he reaches out,
Before the unknown door.
Slowly . . . trembling . . .
An owl calls from a distant place,
Its prey in its claw.
Slowly . . . trembling . . .
The lock clicks, the hinges creak,
The door swings open wide.
Slowly . . . trembling . . .
Now the next time you open your eyes,
Fear is by your side.
Slowly . . . trembling . . .

Eleanor Chappell (12)
Cranford House School, Wallingford

The Winter Evening Settles

The winter evening settles as the sunset fades
Roaring red fires laugh raucously round the room
Curtains peep open in a slight breeze
As comfy chairs slouch around the room
Duvets struggle to snuggle, ready for the story to be told
Teddies cuddle up while the winter evening settles.

Amy Sansom (11)
Cranford House School, Wallingford

Relief

Relief is walking away from a problem
Dropping a huge weight
Relief is glowing with rays of sunlight
Arriving on time for a date

Relief sweeps through the sweltering desert
As a gush of cool wind
Relief is a pair of welcoming arms
When you know that you have sinned

Relief is a lost dog bounding home to its owner
Puffing and panting with glee
Relief is sunlight beaming through the clouds
And shimmering on the sea

Relief is waking from an awful nightmare
Snuggling down in your bed
Relief is a pack of soothing ice
When you've fallen and bashed your head.

Lauren Field (12)
Cranford House School, Wallingford

The Sunset Is Setting

The sunset is fading through the curtains
Daylight has nearly gone ready for tomorrow
I can see the colours, muted and blind
Half the sun has gone, only little light left
A tired sun ready for bed
Blinds drawn
No light seen, only tomorrow.

Esther Irving (11)
Cranford House School, Wallingford

Happiness

Happiness is a day of sunshine,
Glittering in the light.
Happiness is for you and me,
To snuggle up at night.

Happiness is a freshly cut lawn,
And the smell of burning bonfires.
Happiness is honesty,
Truthfulness, not lies.

Happiness is a guiding star,
Reflecting from sea to sea.
Happiness is a treasure hunt,
Looking for the enchanted key.

Happiness is a joy of laughter,
When the bottle of champagne pops!
Happiness is when everything's clean,
Sliding into a new pair of socks.

Happiness is a newborn baby,
Spreading smiles over people's faces.
Happiness is a new pair of shoes,
When tying up their laces.

Happiness brings the whole world together,
With love and consideration.
Happiness is working together,
That's what makes a nation.

Poppy Jackson (11)
Cranford House School, Wallingford

Confusion

Confusion is an unknown language
Being read from an unknown book.

Confusion is a young girl
Who is first learning to cook.

Confusion is an empty fog
Searching for something unseen.

Confusion is a lost boy
In woods where no one else has been.

Confusion is an empty street
Where you are walking alone.

Confusion is a little lamb
A long way away from home.

Confusion is a pair of twins
Who are the same in every small way.

Confusion is an empty space
Which changes every day.

Confusion is a blizzard of questions
Directing the words to your ear.

Confusion is a deaf man
Being read this poem when he can't hear.

Rebekah Donald (12)
Cranford House School, Wallingford

Mystery . . .

He stays in the dark street all night long,
Neither moving nor talking, just standing around.

If you dare to look, you see one side of his face,
A man in profile from an unknown race.

Start to read, mingle with the story,
The intention is living in the character's glory.

A rap at the door breaks your concentration,
It spoils the character's unique animations.

Go downstairs to unlock the door,
But the visitor is gone, he is no more.

Ambling upstairs, return to the room,
But this will reveal to you your awaiting doom.

The book is gone, the ending is barred,
You shall now be forever scarred.

For without the key to the mystery, your soul is gone,
You will no longer be.

Rosie Miller (11)
Cranford House School, Wallingford

The Wood

In the dark and lonely wood
A menacing figure glared into the trees
Silently
Slithering through the wood he went
As the wind whistled under his breath
He reached a lake
Black like death
Where there had been so many deaths before.

Paige Lingwood (12)
Cranford House School, Wallingford

Frustration

Frustration is trying to get someone to listen to your woes
You cry at night
Get into fights
And no one really knows

Frustration is trying to say what you mean
When you're under pressure
You try to talk
But instead you walk
Off in search of leisure

Frustration is trying to write a poem with a single thought
Your words don't go
Your rhymes don't flow
And *you* end up with nought!

Katrina Allen (13)
Cranford House School, Wallingford

Cappuccino

It swirls like whirlwind when it's done,
A drizzle of milk for a perfect dream,
Fresh coffee beans with an extra stir,
And melted chocolate with a dollop of cream.

Heat up the water, let it boil,
Pour it out and froth it up,
Add the milk, and beans, and cream,
To finish off just drink it up.

Gracie Miller (11)
Cranford House School, Wallingford

Confusion

Confusion is hesitant,
He doesn't know what to do.
His eyes are full of curiosity
And tries to see what's going on
But nothing works at all.

Confusion looks this way and that,
Lost in a world of wonder.
He scratches his head
And still continues to ponder.

Confusion never knows what to say,
If he lets something slip then he might be sent away.
He's a muddle, and all over the place
But he can't get himself together again.

He then explodes with questions,
He needs to know what's going on,
He starts to get angry,
He's all in a fluster,
He's controlling more than he can muster.

Then he starts to settle down,
Slightly upset is he,
Cos knowledgeable
He knows he'll never be.

It's like his sight of knowing
Is covered by fog or clouds,
Drifting, drifting
Slowly without a sound.

Fiona Hildred (12)
Cranford House School, Wallingford

The Sunset Field

The sunset field dozes, drifting off to sleep
As the day starts to end,
The sunset field, colours of the rainbow,
All in its perfect shades,
The day has gone, whispering as the wind blows,
The day has almost ended,
The sunset fades and fades away,
While the sunset sleeps.

Emily Sansom (11)
Cranford House School, Wallingford

The Dark, Deep Woods!

In the dark, deep woods,
Men hide with dark hoods.
The trees cry as the wind rushes by.
The wood fell silent,
The men got violent.
The fog creeps in, engulfing the dead!

Carly Goggin (12)
Cranford House School, Wallingford

The Sea Is A Hungry Dog

The sea is a hungry dog lashing at the rocks
Pouncing upon the shore
The sea is a hungry dog bounding up the cliffs
Crashing onto the sand
The sea is a hungry dog destroying everything in its path.

Genevieve Moody (12)
Cranford House School, Wallingford

We Love Pets

My best friend has a chocolate dog,
Brother Tom has a green, slimy frog,
Auntie Jane has a Siamese cat,
Uncle John has a vampire bat.

A mouse lives with cousin Joe,
A hamster lives with Great Aunt Flo.
Chickens roost in our garden shed,
And I keep a snake underneath my bed.

Pets are important to me and you,
Without them I wonder what we'd do.
But of all the pets, the greatest of all,
Is the crocodile that lives in the hall!

Anna Berrisford (11)
Danley Middle School, Sheerness

Spring

Melt away the ice
Bring on the sun
Tell the winter to go away
Tell it its work is done.

Work your wonder
Work your charm
Change the season
But make no harm.

Shine the sun down on us
Make the flowers grow
Look after the baby lamb
Make all enemies go.

Turn the world around
Turn the sky blue
Make a difference in this life
A difference in me and you.

Angharad Lanning (11)
Danley Middle School, Sheerness

I've Been Watching You, Dad

I've been watching you, Dad,
Since the day I was born,
And this is the conclusion I've made.
Being a dad is a wonderful job,
Even though you don't get paid.

You get to play with excellent toys,
Power drills, sanders and saws.
You are even allowed to mess up the house,
Leaving rubbish all over the floors.

Your home is your kingdom, you rule the remote,
It's duty to be by your side.
Cartoons and war films are all that you watch,
And all female access denied.

Bath time is another adventure for you,
The challenge, how hot can it be?
The water is scalding; your skin is bright red,
How you survive is a puzzle to me.

I hope when I'm older, I can be just like you,
Happy, exciting and fun.
I hope my kids look up to me the way I do you,
It is an honour to be called your son.

Jason Binfield (11)
Danley Middle School, Sheerness

My Family Are Bonkers

My family are bonkers,
Bonkers you know,
They're raving mad I tell you,
But they're very polite though.

First of all there's mad Dad,
Mad Dad you know,
His shed is his second home,
And he has an extra toe!

Then there is crazy Mum,
Crazy Mum you know,
Tesco and back, Tesco and back,
Like a really fast yo-yo!

Next there is good old me,
Good old me you know,
I'm the only uncrazy one,
But I have my moments though.

My family are bonkers,
Bonkers you know,
Oh no please, please, please don't do that!
They're strangling Michael O!

Thomas Cantellow (11)
Danley Middle School, Sheerness

Wind

The wind, unlike other ladies
Does not say please and thank you
Does not queue up outside shops
But she does push, shove and be rude
That's why she's got no friends.

The wind is a loud monster
Bending through grass, plants and trees
Thundering past people in the street
Wearing flowing gowns of silver
Long hair of blonde drapes her back.

Bracelets and necklaces of gold litter her body
She talks to trees as she passes
The grass trembles as she goes by
But the rain needs her help
As she also covers the Earth.

Wind has got a bad personality
She's bossy, noisy and bad-tempered
But she is good-looking and funny
She hasn't had a boyfriend yet
Apart from Snow, but he froze her up.

Jade Charles (11)
Danley Middle School, Sheerness

Serial Killer

Resplendent in mink, my cat called Jasper,
He's a serial killer I said,
For he'll catch a bird and will bring it in dead.

You wouldn't think he could,
But you should watch him leap in the air,
Birds beware!

Jasper is slothful but energetic at will,
Sometimes he'll flop and stall,
When we try and move him from the hall.

As he waves his tail gracefully,
Acting so very coy, when lying on
his back with his paws extended,
Nobody knows what is intended.

Jasper pads along the fences with
Extraordinarily large paws,
He is winsome so our neighbours
often mistake him for a girl,
They say he's as desirable as a pearl.

Jasper hunts all types of birds,
So we keep track of his catches,
Make sure nothing hatches.

Some people think he isn't but I
know that he is a thriller, a chiller,
A serial killer!

Katelin Thomas (11)
Danley Middle School, Sheerness

My Journey Through The Year

Spring is kind, she is bouncy but gentle,
She gives the crocuses their wake-up call and then bounces off.
She sews the little lambs their first coat
And gives the little bunnies their first bounce!

Winter lays down his duvet of white as children play in the snow,
Winter is cold and nasty at heart,
Yet he is stubborn and will not get up until late in the day.

Summer spreads her rays upon the sands
And makes the water glisten like mirrors.
She wakes the birds early and they burst into tune.
She makes our days longer and time passes slowly.
She makes us wait in anticipation for her grand finale, sunset.

Autumn wraps her golden, crisp leaves around her like a gown.
She goes to bed earlier than summer,
Then she covers the world in her blanket of dusk.
She leaves it later to paint her sunrise.

Faye Saunders (11)
Danley Middle School, Sheerness

Daisy Chain

I am a daisy chain,
Long and pale,
I am sweet and comforting,
Delicate and can be easily broken.

Very fragile and beautiful,
I can be as long or as short as you wish,
I can bring you joy and happiness,
A token of affection from one to another.

Jessica Dawson (12)
Dunottar School, Reigate

This Tale Of Woe

(A poem in response to Andrew Marvell's 'To His Coy Mistress')

In response to your latest daft attempt,
I'd like to say your mind's completely bent.
Coyness is most certainly not a crime,
But how dare you insinuate that the crime is mine?
I may sit and contemplate,
But after all this time it's far too late.
I may walk past on long love's day,
But I will be going the opposite way.
Your vegetable love may have grown,
But all your attempts you've gone and blown.
I may only show my heart at the last age,
But I shall never get to that final page.
You may call this love undoubted fate,
But I cannot love you at any rate.
Time's winged chariot is hurrying near,
But the petrol prices are far too dear.
Deserts may go on for vast eternities,
But I will die away before you end your ghastly deeds.

The way you spoke in your previous letter,
Shows me you can charm much better,
And because of this,
I see that the one tempting is not me.
Last week when we met,
I would have laid a bet,
On the thought of us working out,
But now I have a serious doubt.
When I told you of these thoughts that had begun to show,
You became my greatest foe,
And now I live in fear,
And nothing I say you ever hear.
Although I'd like to say,
That next Wednesday,
I would come and put things right,
I can't for I must take flight.
I'm sorry for any anger I have caused,
But you brought it on yourself as I felt much too forced.

Now, however, I must admit,
That I may be having thoughts to commit,
And spend my life in this insanity,
And I am not holding myself in any kind of vanity,
For you have placed me high up in your mind,
And I am frightened I may not be so kind.
So therefore it is with regret that I leave,
And on no account should you start to grieve,
For I will be long gone by your next calling,
And please just quit all of this stalling,
As I am now leaving you far, far behind,
For the light in my head brighter than ever it shined,
And now I have left forever,
No moral can bring us back together,
For I am now dead, buried, gone,
But my love for you cannot be reborn,
But I will never know,
And so ends this tale of woe.

Verity Lambert (14)
Dunottar School, Reigate

Miss Lightning And Miss Moon

It was the middle of the night,
Miss Lightning was having a rage,
With her blazing face and upturned chin.
Miss Moon tried to comfort her,
With her kind and glowing personality,
But Miss Lightning gave her a strike.
Miss Moon slid behind a passing cloud,
But Miss Lightning could still see her,
As she was still full.
Miss Lightning was calming down,
And was sorry for the crater she had given Miss Moon.
Miss Moon was now less frightened,
And peeped out from behind a cloud.
All that could be seen,
Was her beautiful, blushing face.

Megan Clarke (12)
Dunottar School, Reigate

This War

A Black Watch soldier killed
On a road to a new base
He was found as a dead man
Officials won't reveal his face.

He was the only one who was killed
Three other men were involved
They only had minor wounds
He died in his tank so cold.

At the same time in Iraq
A bomb had exploded
When the English did arrive
It felt like their guns were loaded.

Heavy vehicles now are trapped
They are down under piles of sand
Three bombs have gone off now
More troops are needed to lend a hand.

This war is so confusing
I just wish that it would end
Think of all the Iraqis dead
Iraq is turning round the bend.

Beatrice Kerslake (12)
Dunottar School, Reigate

Fear

Fear is like lightning
A shock in the stomach.
A horrible feeling
Fear stays inside you, it strikes
Your stomach feels tight
Like a sharp knife inside.
You feel scared, you feel alone
Nobody can help you
Because fear won't go away!

Emma Telford (12)
Dunottar School, Reigate

Love

Love smells like freshly-baked bread,
Fresh blossom in spring,
A crisp, new morning.
Love looks like the first leaf to fall in autumn,
The first dewdrop on the grass in the morning,
The first smile of a baby.
Love tastes like ice cream on a hot day,
A refreshing glass of orange juice in the sun,
A bowl of peaches and cream.
Love feels like a hot shower in the morning,
A velvet dress,
The bristles of a hairbrush.
Love sounds like sleigh bells ringing on Christmas Eve,
A bird singing in the morning,
A romantic song on Valentine's Day.
Love is the best thing in the world,
Love is what created this world.
What will end it?

Ashling Ramdin (11)
Dunottar School, Reigate

Anger

Fire is like anger,
Suddenly lashing out,
Clueless, not knowing what to do next.
The steam is like anger coming off his face,
The cheeks exploding like sparks hitting the floor,
The aggression punching the pillow,
Just like fire crackling on the ground,
Shouting like the roar of the fire erupting.
The water over the flames like tears falling off the face,
The flames fade just as the head does
When it hits the pillow exhausted.

Charlotte Hutchinson (11)
Dunottar School, Reigate

Abandoned

The puppy cried in the corner of the cage
People stared through the window like he was on stage
But nobody wanted to take him home
This poor little puppy, sad and alone.

One little girl stopped to stare
And said, 'Mummy, I want that one there.'
So she took him home and named him Andy
And she made him look so fresh and dandy.

But Andy needed lots of affection
And she never gave him any attention
She didn't even notice that one day
Her dad took the puppy far, far away.

He tied him to a chain link fence
And left him there with no defence
The whole night long he whimpered and whined
As he was left there for no one to find.

But in the morning when he was forlorn
Along came an old lady called Dawn
She cuddled him and took him home
And fed him sausages and meat with a bone.

She looked for a tag but there wasn't one there
He turned up to her and gave her a stare
His puppy-dog eyes were too much to bend
So she kept him forever. What a happy end.

Victoria Godefroy (12)
Dunottar School, Reigate

The Twin Towers

The day was cool and crisp and bright,
The passengers calmly boarded their flight.
The street was busy, frantic and filled,
The workers continued their daily drill.

The planes took off, coffee was served,
The papers unfolded with cool reserve.
The computers turned on, buzz and noise,
No one could know that disaster was poised.

Coffee was spilt, computers died,
Passengers and workers shouted and cried.
The stairs were blocked, twin towers too tall,
The rescue services could not help at all.

The sky turned dark, air full of smoke,
The frantic world stood still and watched and hoped.
The cries below and above surround,
The horror of buildings collapsed around.

The day was dark and bleak and cold,
The scared families left had to be told.
The streets were full of rubble and dust,
How could these cruel people do this to us?

Zoe Case-Green (12)
Dunottar School, Reigate

Red Berries - Haiku

Rich, red berries hang,
So small but catches the eye,
Colour floods the woods.

Nadia Harper (11)
Dunottar School, Reigate

The Aberfan Disaster

Have you heard of the Aberfan disaster?
A waste tip slid down a hillside
It happened in the mining village of Aberfan
One hundred and forty-four people died.

It occurred on the 21st of October
Nearly 40 years ago
It came down on a cottage then Pantglas School
The last day of school at 9.15 was full of woe.

First the roof came flying off!
Then the walls gave way
The whole school turned to rubble
Too fast, too quick to run away.

No one saw anything
But all certainly heard a crash;
Everyone rushed towards the noise
And there they saw the hillside had a big gash.

People came from different counties
They heard what had happened on the news
People only wanted to help
But all they found were a pair of shoes.

A week ago the accident had occurred
One hundred and sixteen children died
All the rescue attempts were futile
The whole of Wales sighed.

Carolyn Bullimore (11)
Dunottar School, Reigate

Thunder V Lightning

Lightning wore a tight yellow top and trousers
She leapt at high speed
Her hair was spiky

Thunder wore a baggy grey pair of dungarees
He was loud and travelled with heavy footsteps
His hair was never neat

Lightning jumped
The whole sky lit up
She took her position
Thunder rumbled
Towards her, the whole Earth shook

Lightning stood still
Then with one flash
Hit Thunder and threw his power away

Thunder raged with anger
He ran towards his enemy
He turned and grew weaker

Lightning twisted and turned
Thunder ran and rolled
Crash!
Lightning leaped onto Thunder
And the sky blazed with light
And Lightning claimed her victory.

Joanna Childs (11)
Dunottar School, Reigate

Rainbow Haikus

The colour of death
As the Devil approaches
He's ready to kill.

Leaves drop from a tree
A burst of orange floats down
Autumn has arrived.

Sun watches the world
Keeping all the rain away
Sunny, yellow day.

Green for the army
The colour that protects us
When we are at war.

The sky when it's hot
Maybe a small swirl of cloud
The weather we like.

Indigo at dawn
Burst of colour fills the sky
As the cockerel crows.

Plum on the table
A lovely, big, juicy fruit
There to be eaten.

Sarah Clement (12)
Dunottar School, Reigate

I Am . . .

I'm a piece of paper,
I'm kind and sensitive,
People write all over me,
I'm good for doing homework on.

I'm stuck up everywhere,
I sometimes get ripped up,
I'm shy and quiet,
But I sometimes cut people,
I'm one of the most useful things you'll find.

My best friend is ink,
I come in all different shapes, sizes and colours,
Scissors are my enemy,
So please keep them away from me.

Madeleine Stansfeld (12)
Dunottar School, Reigate

I Am . . .

I am a snowflake
Dainty as a ballerina,
Sailing through the air
Silent as a mouse
Creeping through a home.
I don't like the summer
And the pollinated flowers,
Summer makes me melt.
I stay with winter
And all the snow
Being cold and freezing
Is winter's glow.

Sophie Flanagan (12)
Dunottar School, Reigate

Pathway To Heaven

Have you seen that glimmer of light
Waiting for you, sparkling bright?
You may be weak and on your knees
But get to the light and your pain will ease.
It hovers on golden wings of hope
To reach and send you a lifeline, a rope.
Cling to the rope, you will be saved
Your pathway to Heaven has been paved.

Rosean Fernando (14)
Enfield County School, Enfield

Life

Life is full of hate
Life is something that will go out of date
Life is just a fear for you to overcome
Life is just something for you and someone
Life is full of dreams waiting to be fulfilled
Life is like a wound waiting to be healed
Life is full of hope and fears
Life is like a pool full of tears
Life gives us a chance to break free
Life gives us a chance to feel free
Life can be a saying or a word
Life can be hurt and unheard
Life is full of qualities and features
Life is taught by you and your teachers
Life is not to be wasted
Life is something, just face it
Life . . .

Adam Rutstein (15)
JFS School, Kenton

The Nymph

Running through a forest,
Falling to the ground.
Suddenly my gaze caressed,
The captivating figure that was found.
Stumbling to my feet,
Unable to shift my glare.
My heart thumping at a rising beat,
As my eyes settled on this creature, pure and fair.
She floated by my side,
And kissed me there and then.
My heart stopped . . . I almost died,
But then my strength returned to defeat all men.
She made me weak,
I was paralysed.
I could not speak,
I could not be revived,
For I was in a world of my own.
She opened my eyes to see,
That I would never be alone,
As long as she remained with me.
But as the dream began,
The dawning of all purpose occurred,
And as she hummed, as she sang,
She seemed to forget her word.
Then I tried to hold her,
She took one step back.
But then she froze and did not stir,
And then my world turned black.
She fell to pieces, I watched in horror,
And my heart began to sink.
She turned to dust, as did my honour,
And my happiness gone with a single blink.
And as I watched her float away,
She ended and she started.
And as I joined her fate to say,
Never again shall we be parted.

Claudia Cramer (15)
JFS School, Kenton

The Haunted School

In the haunted school, so dark,
You can sometimes hear the sound of a harp.
In the playground the wind whistles,
Through the overgrown field of thistles.

You can always hear thunder,
Why? I've always wondered.
The moon glistens through the field,
People who have come here have been killed.

The classrooms have a smell,
Because of the people who have gone to Hell.
Floorboards creak as I walk,
While you can hear ghosts talk.

When I pick up the pencil,
I draw something with the stencils.
I see something in the distance,
Don't worry, it was only a sixpence!

I see a something in the classroom.
It's a figure in the corner.
I've actually seen a . . .
Ghost!

Taylor Ann Davies (11)
King Ethelbert School, Birchington

I Ride My Horse

I ride my horse through the fields
I ride my horse like nothing is going to bother us
I ride my horse morning 'til night
I ride my horse every day.

Kirsty Reed (13)
King Ethelbert School, Birchington

School

Children learnin'
Teachers earnin'
Minds thinkin'
Students linkin'
Test takin'
Hand shakin'
Mornin' greetin'
Dinner eatin'
Pen clickin'
Clock tickin'
Hand raisin'
Teacher praisin'
Story tellin'
Pupils yellin'
Bell ringin'
Children singin'
Friends blendin'
Poem endin'.

Christian Meah (11)
King Ethelbert School, Birchington

Old Man Poem

White hair, white hair
Wrinkly face and frail
Do you see the sunshine?
Your face is so pale
Do you go for a walk somewhere
Where the dogs bark and children play?
That will put a smile on your face
And you will look forward to another day.

Hannah Alexandrou (12)
King Ethelbert School, Birchington

Spell Poem

(Inspired by 'Macbeth')

We are the three horrible witches,
We are no good and make lots of hitches.

Bubble, bubble soil and rubble,
Let the lady burn and the water bubble.
We don't care,
So don't you glare.

We are the three horrible witches,
We are no good and make lots of hitches.

Tail of a rat,
Claw of a cat,
Skin of a snake,
And let it bake.

This is what you need to make the potion,
As soon as it touches your lips there will be no motion.

Drink it up, you know you wanna,
Once inside you're a gonner.

Aaa ha ha ha!

Owen Connolly (14)
King Ethelbert School, Birchington

Dying

Dying
Last breath
Shiver down spine
Say your last word
Dead.

John Dean (12)
King Ethelbert School, Birchington

The Story Of A Stuck Up Kitten

Have you ever heard of a cat
Who sticks her nose up at chicken?
She sits there,
Waiting for more food,
Watching the clock go tickin'.

She walks around,
Looking proud,
Thinking she's the cat's miaow.
Our other cats get annoyed
For they are older than her.
They cannot stand to see her stalk,
Walk or even purr.

Cleo's a queen,
She's posher than you've ever seen.
'I love you, Cleo,' everyone says
But don't let her get you fooled.
She'll pull a trick on you,
Bigger than she's ever pulled . . .

Alyce Cronk (12)
King Ethelbert School, Birchington

Hallowe'en

H allowe'en is a spooky time
A nd the witches give blood saying it's wine
L onely you do not want to be
L ip-smacking vampires you may see
'O rrible werewolves give a terrible bite
W atch out, you may get a very big fright
E ven Dracula has a friend on his arm
E very attempt to keep from harm
N ow beware, you have been warned!

Nicola Baldwin (12)
King Ethelbert School, Birchington

The Horrid Teacher

There once was a teacher at school,
We called her Mrs Cruel,
She stood there all day,
And would always say,
'Shut up and obey my rule!'

We would never play,
As she would say,
'I don't believe in a fun day.'

We don't know anything about her,
No one would dare talk to her.

At the end of the day
She would mutter these words that no one hears,
    Picks up her bags
        And
            Disappears . . .

Danielle Neat (12)
King Ethelbert School, Birchington

Everything We Do!

Flowers blooming,
People talking,
Birds flying,
Children walking.

Builders building,
Birds singing,
Dogs barking,
Teachers thinking.

All these things people do,
Are just the same as *me* and *you!*

Samantha Bale (12)
King Ethelbert School, Birchington

Spell Poem

(Inspired by 'Macbeth')

Boiling in the charmed pot
All the dead man's toes that we've got
An old cat's paw
And a dirty leopard's claw
In the cauldron, boil and bake
Then the eye of a rattlesnake
Eye of newt and leg of frog
And the hairy head of a warthog
Add a ginger cat
Maybe a semi-bald cat
A fat man's sweat
Then a little girl's pet

As the potion boils and simmers
The colour red gets dimmer and dimmer
The bubbles rise then go *pop*
Then the heat rises then drops
Will it work or will it not?
We will see when we look in the pot.

Jamie Saunders (13)
King Ethelbert School, Birchington

A Dolphin Is . . .

A lively hopper
A beautiful animal
A dancing twirler
A shiny ring
A smooth petal from a flower
A wonderful sunset
As fast as a cheetah
A sparkling star
A bright, colourful moon
A slimy snail
A wet penguin.

Tanya Wilson (11)
King Ethelbert School, Birchington

White Rouge

Secret, so secret
He's in the hedgerow
Vroom!
You'll never find him in the snow

Because he's the white rouge of the animal world

He's better than Bond
And MI6
He's secret and stealthy
And full of tricks

Because he's the white rouge of the animal world

He'll be eating grass
Looking innocent then
Bounce, bounce
He'll be on the hutch

So by the way
Now I've had a laugh
I'll tell you what he's really like

He's white, fluffy
With two brown eyes
Munching teeth
He's very wise

So here he is
My little friend
The white rouge of the animal world.

Robert Edwards (12)
King Ethelbert School, Birchington

Witches' Brew

Come, witches,
We've got a potion to brew.
Raven's claw,
More, more and more.

Hear the howling cackles and brew,
As we mix our poisonous stew.

Snake's skin and dragon's egg,
Mushy peas and frog's leg,
Wolf's sharp tooth blade,
Hemlock and deadly nightshade.

Fur of magpie,
And the Devil's eye,
Throw in a spider,
Its legs stretched wider, still wider.

Hear the howling cackles and brew,
As we mix our poisonous stew.

Tiger's heart and scorpion's tail,
Blubber from a giant whale,
Finally a warty toad and wing of bat,
Fish's tails and ear of cat.

Hear the howling cackles and brew,
As we mix our poisonous stew.

Alison Hutchinson (11)
King Ethelbert School, Birchington

Mary's Little Lamb

Mary had a little lamb,
You've heard it all before,
Yet I bet you haven't,
Heard what I've in store!

The lamb was short, piggish and fat,
Its fleece was not snow-white,
It was brown, old and gross,
Stuck down, rough and tight.

Mary kept it in the barn,
Nobody seemed to care,
One day I crept in and,
I saw it sitting there.

I picked it up, what a lump,
Took it to a friend to cook,
Then there it was in the oven,
I bet Mary couldn't cook!

So there you go,
Lamb's a hit,
Mary had a little lamb,
But, yes, I ate it!

Rachael Hammond (13)
King Ethelbert School, Birchington

Sea

Come along, come with me,
Take a dive in the deep blue sea.
Put on your gear, let's explore,
All the way to the ocean floor.

See that snail wrapped in curls?
Look! An oyster wearing pearls!
Watching the octopus, oh so dark,
But do not try to cuddle the shark!

Dive on down, seaward-bound,
Motion in the ocean is all around!
Dive on down, seaward-bound,
Motion in the ocean is all around!

Now we are very far below,
The lantern fish are all aglow.
Is that a tiny shock you feel?
You just met an electric eel!

Giant blue whales start to stir,
Bigger than dinosaurs ever were!
Wave goodbye to the squid and sponge,
This is the end of our deep sea plunge.

Jodie Pashley (12)
King Ethelbert School, Birchington

Spell Poem

(Inspired by 'Macbeth')

There's a spell of evil doings
From 3 witches on a heath,
Fair is foul and foul is fair,
There's evil lingering in the air.

Let me tell you my story
Of the 3 witches on a heath,
It will make you feel quite sick,
With what they put in the cauldron.

The first witch danced around the pot,
And put into their evil brew
A tail of a brown puppy dog
And the nose of a shrew.

The second pulled out of her bag
A boot with a wriggly, white maggot,
And into the pot it went
And then she put in the fire from a firebug.

The third witch put into the pot
A cry from an old, black cat,
A foot of a white rabbit with red eyes,
The soul of a valiant knight.

There's a spell of evil doing
From 3 witches on a heath,
Fair is foul and foul is fair,
There's evil lingering in the air.

Larissa Harrison (13)
King Ethelbert School, Birchington

Black Roses

The children lived in darkness,
Their memories were sad.
They waited until an angel flew,
But their thoughts weren't strong enough.

The evil spell shot into them,
Turned them into spirits.
The black witch turned to them,
Lit a blazed fire.
The cold spirits were lifted into the black, earthy sky,
They flew around to find light to guide them.

But time passed and nothing was achieved,
Their hearts cold and empty.
All around there was no sound,
They were clutched into their soul.
But then it was taken away,
They were advised by the black witch.

Black roses covered the ground,
Trickled into the dark earth.
Their tears were wiped away,
Were sent into a dream to try and release their pain.

Their moods were depressed,
But they thought wrong,
And were guided by the light of an angel.

Katya Derksen (11)
King Ethelbert School, Birchington

Love!

Love is a wonderful feeling,
It makes you hit the ceiling.
The world spins round
When love is found
And it gives you a tingly feeling.

Love brings lots of happiness
But not a lot of stress.
When you're in love
Everything is loved for
And full of tenderness.

Love is a wonderful feeling,
It makes you hit the ceiling.
The world spins round
When love is found
And it gives you a tingly feeling.

Question we, wonderful things about love
Just like, *does he love me*
Or does he not?
Sometimes your love will be as strong as God's heart
And at times the total opposite.

Love is a wonderful feeling,
It makes you hit the ceiling.
The world spins round
When love is found
And gives you a tingly feeling.

Who do you love?
Who do you love?
That is the greatest question!
Once you have found that special person
Keep on loving them with tender care
And tell them you love them!

Courtney Georgina Keenlyside (12)
King Ethelbert School, Birchington

The Zoo

I went to the zoo just a week ago
I thought you ought to know

First we went to see the lions
So strong and bold as can be
Prowling around marking their territory

Creeping, crawling, cunning spiders
Scutter around in their cage
I don't like the spiders

I went to see the monkeys
Swinging through the trees
Monkeys are my favourite
They're just like me
The way they walk, the way they sleep
And even how they eat their tea

Then we went to the giraffes
Giraffes are big and very tall
But mice are so very small
Graceful and pretty as can be
Well, they are just like me!

Next we visited the big, scary, gnashing, nasty crocodiles
Their evil eyes gleamed upon me
I hate them, I want to go

Then we left all the animals
We said goodbye
We drove away
I hope we come back another day!

Chloe Kennard (12)
King Ethelbert School, Birchington

The Old School

Beneath the cold, black skies,
An old, dusty school lies.
In the classroom the cobwebs lay
Where the children used to play.
The children's lockers stay shut
Because they were jammed with a nut.
Where the children put their bags,
All you can see now is old flags.

Beneath the cold, black skies,
An old, dusty school lies.
The floorboards are all squeaking
And all the doors are creaking.
The children's play area
Is now scarier.
There are old, blue chairs
Where a blackbird stares.

Beneath the cold, black skies,
An old, dusty school lies.
The gates are all shut
And that is how it's going to stay.

Jasmine Duggan (11)
King Ethelbert School, Birchington

Love

Love is a wonderful thing,
Love makes the world go on,
Love makes you want to sing
A very happy song.

Love makes you want to jump up to the sky,
Love makes you want to cry,
And makes you want to jump high
Into the bright blue sky.

Love is a good feeling,
And love has very good healing.

Tara May (12)
King Ethelbert School, Birchington

Under The Sea

The giant blue hand stretches across
And grasps the pebbles within
Hissing of waves, howling of wind
We imagine what it's like beneath.

From the elegance of dolphins
To the violence of a shark
The sea is a marvellous mismatch
Of various extraordinary extremes.

Underneath the swirling, swishing waves
The sea is busy with teeming life
Coral reef aglow with shape and colour
As fabulous fish weave in and out and in and out.

Prowling predators lurk in search
Of smaller fish to cold-bloodedly devour
A shark as fierce as a mythical dragon
All part of the watery, flowing sea.

Isabelle Hart (12)
King Ethelbert School, Birchington

Haunted House

In the dead of the night
You hear dead people's groans
And out of nowhere the floorboards creak
The wind blows and howls.

When you go to sleep at night, doors open randomly
The groans get louder!
The creaks get louder!
Then . . . silence!

You go to close the window
There, in front of you, is a white figure
It makes you jump and disappears
That's when you know your house is haunted.

Chris Clements (13)
King Ethelbert School, Birchington

The Haunted House

Underneath the curtain of trees
Lies the dark house
Where ghosts fly around like wisps of wind
And howl like dogs at night.

And the mice fly around like pellets from a gun
Wondering what's around the corner
Where vampires come and go as they please
Hunting at night and sleeping at day.

The creepy headstones which surround the house
Have mould crawling up the side
And the grass is as long as the headstones
With dead flowers spotted around the garden.

The house is almost as dark as the sky at night
With overgrown vine covering one side of the house
The old, moulded door is big and tall
If you look closely you can see strange faces.

People won't go within a mile of the house
Because of the screams and howls
Which send a shiver down your spine
Would you pay a visit to the haunted house?

Emma Rickman (11)
King Ethelbert School, Birchington

Ferraris

F ast cars, lots of speed.
E normous engines, what we need.
R evvin' up really loud.
R eally nice car, I'm very proud.
A nd in the F50 we go cruisin'
R ight along the seafront, all the gamblers losin'.
I n the end my cruise is over.
S tep out of my F50, get into my Rover.

Reece Kurmman (13)
King Ethelbert School, Birchington

Spell Poem

(Based on 'Macbeth')

Again we four witches meet,
Our cauldron sitting by our feet.
'Double, double toil and trouble,
Fire burn and cauldron bubble.'

Add the eye of frog,
Nose of dog,
The shiny scales of a snake,
Then let the cauldron bubble and bake.

Stir the mixture nice and slow,
Then add the tongue of a lizard and a toe.
'Double, double toil and trouble,
Fire burn and cauldron bubble.'

Then wait for a bang and puff of smoke,
Then put in some rat's skin and let it soak.
We're almost done,
But we're still going to have fun!

The potion is now ready to drink.
What do you think?

Jessica Longley (13)
King Ethelbert School, Birchington

The Winter Storm

In November fireworks shine bright
As fires glow on the windy night
Rain pelting roofs, deafening on the winter's night

In December Christmas lights shine and bells chime
Turkey roasting and children boasting
People eating and greeting

In January the snow is falling everywhere
Taking down decorations
Wrapped up warm in the cold.

Joe Andrews (12)
King Ethelbert School, Birchington

Spell Poem

(Based on 'Macbeth')

'Double, double toil and trouble
Fire burn and cauldron bubble'
The 3 witches chant
'Add the flower of a dead plant
Also the ear wax of a snake
And, of course, burnt steak.

Next into the brew
A pig that it knew
Add a pinch of thyme
And the juice of a lime
Also an antelope's brain
That looks like a pink stain.

That is the spell almost done
I'm going to have to add a whale's bum
Add a long, spiny porcupine
And the hand from a climb
What is that?
Now add the wings of a flying cat.

I feel it's time to add a handful of dust
Now a hairy bat, this I must
Add a crocodile's eye
And a chicken pie
Also frog's snot
And last of all 2 blood clots.

Double, double toil and trouble
Fire burn and cauldron bubble
That is our spell completely finished
Now you shall be perished
Double, double toil and trouble
Fire burn and cauldron bubble'.

Natalie O'Connell (14)
King Ethelbert School, Birchington

Falling

I'm falling.
Am I dying?
Am I flying?
I don't know what happened.
Did that bully get to me?
I'm falling.

I'm falling.
Have I died
Or am I dying?
Have I flown
Or am I flying?
Help me! Help me!
I'm falling.

I'm falling.
Am I falling fast or slow?
Will I fall in sand or snow?
Will I go to Heaven
Or will I go to Hell?
I'm falling.

I'm falling.
Will someone catch me?
Will anybody miss me?
Would I fall in a busy high street
Or even in the lonely woods?
I'm falling.
Help *meee!*

Lauren Harris-Murray (13)
King Ethelbert School, Birchington

The Potion

(Inspired by the witches in Shakespeare's 'Macbeth')

'Tis time for the making,
Let it be shaking.
Items from the earth below,
Venom squeezed from a fellow.
Night and day we pray
For the things we say.

Proceed to the cauldron,
Making the potion.

Gut of the greenest snake,
Four fish from the lake,
Eye of a English frog,
Tail of a skinny dog,
Beak of a powerful gull,
Stirring it all so well.

Proceed to the cauldron,
Making the potion.

A hamster's tail
Which has gone round a wheel,
Wax of a cheetah's ear,
Like one full of fear,
Egg of a crocodile's nest.
Burn it, boil it, break it.

Katie Longden (13)
King Ethelbert School, Birchington

The Old School

In the dark, dark night
Where the old school stood
It was so, so spooky
With the floorboards creaking
And all the thick pipes leaking

Then there was silence . . .
The clock struck 12
And it went all quiet
There was not even a squeak from a mouse
Or the floorboards creaking

Then the school entrance opened!
And the wind blew through
And the ghosts came in ready for another day of school
But wailing through the corridor
Making such a racket
Saying weird things
Throwing bits of paper
And trying to sing

Then it was nearly time to go
So the ghosts went home to their graves
And the old school closed
But it's never to be told
That the old school's going to be sold
And reopened again.

Ellie Gillman (12)
King Ethelbert School, Birchington

Little Africa

People get bullied,
For the colour of their skin,
No matter how hard they try,
They can never win.

There's a new girl in my class,
Who comes from far away,
Who is coloured and small,
And gets teased every day.

Some other girls in my class,
Yank and pull her hair,
Kick and spit at her,
And all I do is stare.

Little Africa is her nickname,
They tore up her book,
Kicked around her bag,
And all I did was look.

I wish I could just do something,
Make this cruelty end,
But I know if I interfere,
They'd make my nose bend.

This morning my mum told me,
A girl tied a rope below her head,
Tightened it carefully,
And hung herself from her bunk bed.

So I ran to school the next day,
I really didn't care,
I was going to stick up for her,
But Little Africa wasn't there . . .

Emily Robinson (12)
King Ethelbert School, Birchington

My Hidden Feelings

My hidden feelings I can't describe,
All floating around, trapped inside.
I want to let them out, I really do,
But I can't, my brain is saying through and through.

My friends keep asking what's wrong?
But I say nothing, my feelings are too strong.
Sometimes I wonder over and over again,
I know it will come out, the question is when?

I walk around school feeling lonely and sad,
But everyone just stares like I'm going mad.
No one understands, they never will,
It's just something that they'll never feel.

I want someone to open my heart,
So my feelings can just burst apart.
Someone who has that special key,
To open my feelings inside of me!

Jodie Whittle (13)
King Ethelbert School, Birchington

Winter

The snow is falling from the sky,
Children playing in the snow,
Making snowmen from the snow,
Sledging down the snowy hills.
It gets dark quick, now it's time to go inside
For hot chocolate in front of the fire.

Christmas is this type of season,
In the night all the presents are laid
And in the morning children play with their new toys
Taking them outside
Showing all their friends and playing in the snow.
Now time for a new celebration
Now the *new year is here*.

Lucy Goddard (11)
King Ethelbert School, Birchington

The Haunted Celeb Mansion

Thunder roaring as I run
Upstairs and downstairs
The storm has just begun
There is a noise coming from the cellar
I hope it is Uri Geller

I'm frightened and really scared
As I creep down the stairs
There's a figure standing right there
I hope it's not Tony Blair

As I run out the door
It's night no more, it's nearly dawn
Thank you, Jesus Christ
Look, there's Katie Price.

Ashley Charman (12)
King Ethelbert School, Birchington

The Summer Holiday

1, 2, 3, 4
No need for learning anymore.
A, B, C, D
No teachers left to moan at me.
2, 4, 6, 8
On the beach, I just can't wait.
R, S, T, U
No more homework left to do.
W, X, Y, Z
There's no school so I'm in bed.
3, 5, 7, 9
All my friends come round to mine.
B, C, D, E
We all sit down and watch TV
8, 9, 10, 11
The holiday is pure Heaven.

Amy Collins (12)
King Ethelbert School, Birchington

Dusk

Quick! Run!
Night has begun!
Creatures lurking!
Look! There's one!

Quick! Hide!
Under the slide!
It'll eat you up!
And your pride!

Quick! Look!
The midnight crook!
Boiling cauldrons!
They're ready to cook!

Quick! Mark!
We're in the dark!
Pointy edges!
Jagged bark!

Quick! Wait!
It's getting late!
The horizon's fading!
Goodnight mate!

Lannah-Rose Marshall (13)
King Ethelbert School, Birchington

Black Cat

A black cat comes out at night
Walks across the wall
The moon comes out and shines its light
The cat walks across
As the cat walks you see a shadow
So the black cat is tired now
And the cat goes inside
To its pitch-black bed.

Kelly Moore (13)
King Ethelbert School, Birchington

Being A Teen

I am a teen
An in-between
Not still a kiddy
Not an old biddy
Spotty skin
Greasy hair
Sometimes problems are
Too much to bear
Want to go out
Don't want to stay in
Wanna go where all
My mates have been
Trainers and trackies
Scrunchies and clips
Make-up and bling-bling
Pizza and chips
Discos and shopping
Shopping's a dream
That's what I love
About being a teen!

Kayleigh Glover (13)
King Ethelbert School, Birchington

Weathers

Snow, snow, falling down,
Happiness is all around,
Knock, knock, time for school

Friends waiting at the door,
The sun is out, we want more.
Zoom, zoom, walk to school.

Charlotte Anderson (12)
King Ethelbert School, Birchington

The Haunted House

The girl walks up the stairs
With the mouldy floorboards creaking
She can hear her feet tapping
And can hear the door screeching

As she gets to the top of the stairs
She looks at another creepy thing
She walks slowly in a big, scary room
Where a fat lady sits and sings

She looks at her ugly face
Then the fat lady stops
Then in a horrible voice she said,
'Oh darling, may you go to the shops?'

This girl ran as fast as she could
Down the creaking stairs
Running through the field
With her tiny black flares.

Now that was the end of the fat lady
But she never will be forgotten
Her soul is still there!

Laura Dean (11)
King Ethelbert School, Birchington

Flowers

One lilac lily lounging on a lake
Two red roses reaching really high
Three dropping daisies dragging on the ground
Four bright bluebells blowing in the breeze
Five tall tulips towering tall as can be
Six shiny sunflowers standing like a soldier.

Flowers, flowers everywhere.

Amber Hallett (11)
King Ethelbert School, Birchington

The Ocean's Current!

Swish, swosh, swish, swosh goes the sea.
The dark and cold water bashing against the rocks.
As I enter the water it comes up to my knees
And my woolly socks.

The current takes me out.
Waves push against me.
Around a boat that knocks me about,
As I float out to sea.

My teeth chittering-chattering,
The ice-cold water freezing me.
Now the rain starts *splish splosh splashing,*
As I float out to sea.

Now it is dark, the moon shining,
Only an artificial light shining on me.
I can hear thunder, thunder and lightning,
As I float out to sea.

Day is dawning and I'm yawning
And I can see land not too far from me.
As I swim, swim with the energy I have left
But the current is too strong and takes me back out to sea.

Harley Dennis (12)
King Ethelbert School, Birchington

The Cemetery

(Inspired by 'The Raven' by Edgar Allan Poe)

I walked into the cemetery,
It was as silent as the dead,
Suddenly I heard a tapping,
As someone gently rapping,
Rapping at their chamber door.

I followed the sound,
Treading over the bumpy ground,
Around a tomb,
Another and another,
The journey took forever.

The sound grew louder,
A mumble and a thud,
Didn't want to go there,
Didn't need a scare.

I reached the sound,
On freshly dug ground,
'Hello?' I said and waited.
'I'm down here,' it said,
'They thought I was dead - I'm not,
I just don't snore!'

Peter Lane (13)
King Ethelbert School, Birchington

Dragon's Fire

Dragon's fire, traitor, liar
In town and city, mountain, glen,
His black scales glitter in the light of the fire,
Bright eyes shining like diamonds upon dirt,
Anger rises like lava in a volcano,
Blasts a red-hot flame at a once great king,
Spreads his powerful wings to the width of a mountain,
Flying at impossible speeds,
To his home,
A treasure hoard.

He is the fear of all that live,
A ghost of a long-lost past.
Traitors, liars, sent to the dragon's den,
Prove their worth or die in the end.
Armies of men trained for the purpose
Of destroying a beast as old as the hills.
Those who try will fail,
For all his years he has learned
To breathe ice and fire.
Nothing may pierce his once great, dark scales,
His deep, jagged teeth are as sharp as any sword,
The knowledge he possesses is greater than any man or beast.

So a message to all those who care to listen,
Beware the dragon whose black scales glisten.
For he will be the last thing you ever see.
(Young children must learn
The end of those who lie and cheat
Are the lowest of lows.)

Teagan A Pallett (13)
King Ethelbert School, Birchington

The Haunted House

I walked up to the massive door
I opened it, it creaked
I walked in and heard a whistle
I am sure it was a ghost.

I walked up the staircase
It was long and straight
I heard a bang
I am sure it was a ghost.

I got to the top scared
My heart was thumping
I heard a scream
I am sure it was a ghost.

I saw another staircase
It was small and long
I heard a ghostly voice
I am sure it was a ghost.

I saw green slime
It made me shiver
I heard a smash
I am sure it was a ghost.

And there it was
In the doorway
White, dead and creepy
It was the ghost!

It was coming towards me
I screamed and yelled, ran and fell
There it was, standing over me
It was, it was *the ghost!*

Benjamin Vernon (12)
King Ethelbert School, Birchington

The Night Sky

Wolves are howling as the bears are growling
In the night sky
Owls are hooting as the birds are tooting
In the night sky
Cats are pouncing as the rabbits are bouncing
In the night sky

Bats are flying as the night is dying
In the night sky
The ghosts are booing as the clowns are fooling
In the night sky
Badgers are burrowing as the moles are tunnelling
In the night sky

The moon is shining as the sun is rising
In the night sky
It's now day, the night is no longer at bay
In the day sky.

Aiden Ling (12)
King Ethelbert School, Birchington

Sunrise

Sunrise is beautiful,
It's when the birds sing,
Sunrise is calm,
When there's a light slight breeze.

Sunrise is beautiful,
The sky turns pink,
Sunrise is when everyone's asleep.

Then in no time,
Sunrise is gone,
Be back tomorrow,
When it is calm.

Jade Hansford (12)
King Ethelbert School, Birchington

Snow

I colour the grass white, carefully, slowly
I let people make snowballs and chuck them fiercely, delightfully
I am happy when people play with my whiteness joyfully, happily
People get cold hands and faces, freezing, shivering

I carry on falling down from the sky, calmly, surely
I am the weather that allows snowmen to be built, merrily, anxiously
I am the weather that makes people wrap up warm, tightly, warmly
I am the weather that makes animals hibernate

I crunch beneath your feet, slipping, sliding
I turn to ice, skating, gliding
I am the weather that causes accidents, crashing, banging
I only appear now and then but cause chaos, confusion

I slowly start to melt, dripping, dropping
As quickly as I appear, I disappear
I am a lot of fun to play with but I don't last very long
I am snow.

Nathan Pressley (11)
King Ethelbert School, Birchington

Liane

My foster carer Liane
Looks after me the best she can.
Sometimes she shouts at me,
She doesn't eat much tea.
Sometimes she's really fun
And she gives me quite a lot of pocket money.
She's got blonde streaks in her hair
Which gives her quite a flair.
She likes fish and has a fish pond
But she wishes she had a magic wand.
She has a nice garden
And she always says pardon.

Neil Lewis (11)
King Ethelbert School, Birchington

Grandad's Gone

Grandad's gone
Not with us anymore
He was a nice man
Wouldn't hurt a fly

Grandad's gone
Not with us anymore
He was a friendly man
As friendly as can be

Grandad's gone
Not with us anymore
He used to take us to the beach
And get us an ice cream

Grandad's gone
Not with us anymore
He was a great man
And as friendly as can be.

Jake Powell (11)
King Ethelbert School, Birchington

Winter

Leaves are falling on the ground
When they touch they turn all brown
Children playing in the snow
When a strong wind blows

All the animals are hibernating
That's why they're not around
It's getting dark
And still children are playing in the park

Christmas lights are beaming
As children's eyes are gleaming
Christmas songs are playing
As lots of snow is laying.

Sophie Jade Scarsbrook (12)
King Ethelbert School, Birchington

Mighty Jungle

Mighty jungle on the land
Two snakes slithering in the sand
There's a buffalo's nose and some warthogs' toes
But the ferocious lion everyone knows
On his walk he sees:

One wailing wombat wriggling wildly
Two tall tigers tearing tenderly
Three thin falcons flying fiercely
Four fed up ferrets fidgeting frantically
Five fast, frozen fish feeding
Six slithering snakes seeing snails slurp sausages
Seven shivering sheep singing sweetly
Eight eating elephants awoken early
Nine nice nectar birds
Ten tired terrapins treading tiredly.

He also spots a deer in the middle of the field . . .

Zoom! Crunch!
That's why he's the king of the mighty jungle!

Briony Smith (12)
King Ethelbert School, Birchington

Snow Days

Snow, snow, white, white snow.
Snowball fight, lots of good fun.
Snow, snow, white, white snow.

Snow, snow, white, white snow.
Snowman building, lots of fun.
Snow, snow, white, white snow.

Snow, snow, white, white snow.
Making snow angels is fun.
Snow, snow, white, white snow.

Joseph Nightingale (12)
King Ethelbert School, Birchington

The Ghost!

I am the ghost that ohhs and ahhs
I am the ghost that travels so fast
I am the ghost that nobody sees
I am the ghost that makes wobbly knees.

I live in the house of spooks
With my friends all creepy and crawly
I rattle my chains and clatter my chimes
While my friends go off and commit lots of crimes.

I am the ghost that ohhs and ahhs
I am the ghost that travels so fast.

Friday is the night I go spooking
With all my friends we hover
We fly and we fly right up to the sky
And make all the little ones cry.

I am the ghost that ohhs and ahhs
I am the ghost that travels so fast.

I love the smell of the dark night sky
It is so misty and gloomy
All I see are the lights of the houses shining
Bright in my eyes as I travel through the midnight sky.

I am the ghost that ohhs and ahhs
I am the ghost that travels so fast.

My night work is done
When the screaming has sung
And the children are all wide awake
They were just dreaming, it's all make-believing
As I fly and listen to their cries and screaming.
Ha! Ha!

Poppy Keam (12)
King Ethelbert School, Birchington

Dolphins

Dolphins swim in the big blue sea,
They swim, they swim but what can they see?

Clams that are snapping
But look like they're clapping,
Jellyfish's tentacles tingling
So they go off stinging.

The ghost shrimp that's ghostful
But isn't very boastful
And seaweed that's waving
But then it starts fading.

When they swim, when they swim
That's what is seen
By the dolphins that swim
In the big blue sea.

Rebecca Gee (12)
King Ethelbert School, Birchington

Naughty Children

Very naughty children
Who do very naughty things

Like pull cats' tails
And tweak Mum's hair
And hide their sister's hairbrush
And throw things in the air

Now these children are quite naughty
And really don't behave
They make Mummy do her cooking wrong
And Dad miss his shave

Now think very carefully
And think what else they might do
Does it remind you of anyone?
How about *you!*

Melissa Coupland (11)
King Ethelbert School, Birchington

My Great Nan

She was so special to me
I loved her so
But now she is no longer

She was a hip-hop grandma
A funky diva grandma
Always caring
But always forgetting!

She was so special to me
I loved her so
But now she is no longer

A few weeks ago was her funeral
I miss her so
Her name was Anne
She had a Victorian pram
That she kept in her basement

She was so special to me
I loved her so
But now she is no longer

She lived in Ireland
With her children
Her house was lovely
It was a cottage with the view of the countryside
And a car park outside

She was so special to me
I loved her so
But now she is no longer
But I still love her
And I will never forget her.

Jessica Osbourn (12)
King Ethelbert School, Birchington

The Gruesome, Ghastly Witches' Spell

(Based on 'Macbeth')

'Double, double toil and trouble
Fire burn and cauldron bubble'
Placing in a cut-up tie
Plus a bloodshot warthog's eye
Add a leg of a frog
And some smelly earwax of a dog
Sprinkle in rubbings of a rubber
And some sliced up seal's blubber

'Double, double toil and trouble
Fire burn and cauldron bubble'
Throw in some straggly hairs of a tramp's beard
And a tequila worm, oh so weird
Add the springs of a bed
Plus a pencil's silver lead
A handful of a dead animal's fur
A skanky flea-ridden cat that has lost its purr

'Double, double toil and trouble
Fire burn and cauldron bubble'
Add the skin of a dead bat
And the whiskers of a loopy rat
A squirrel's tail
The tongue of a whale
Which is huge, is it not?
For so is our potion's pot.

'Double, double toil and trouble
Fire burn and cauldron bubble'
So add a feather of a bird
And a human's tooth, how absurd
Our cauldron is nearly filled
Our spell is ready, don't want it spilled.

Gemma White (14)
King Ethelbert School, Birchington

By Shadow Of Night!

(Based on 'Macbeth')

On the moor the cloaked hags meet,
Through the rain and heavy sleet.
Wrapped in rags of dirty grey,
In malice and riddle their thoughts do lay.

Their faces hidden by shadow of night,
Wind and rain on their skin do bite.
The cauldron simmers with bubbles of hate,
Macbeth doth approach, his life on their plate.

Fair is foul and foul is fair,
Hover through the fog and filthy air.
All three bleat in chorus of voice,
Ingredients of Hell, here lies their choice.

A withered hand from one cloak doth appear,
Covered with guilt and riddled with fear.
Into a bag her hand doth go,
Like a snake to its prey, her fingers do show.

From her bag she pulls a book,
With recital of words the ground doth shook.
His life in their hands, the apparition hath shown,
King in his coffin, Macbeth to the throne.

'Double, double toil and trouble,
Fire burn and cauldron bubble.'

Andrew Denton (14)
King Ethelbert School, Birchington

Spell Poem!

(Based on 'Macbeth')

Three witches by a cauldron they stand,
Putting in the bloody hand,
All gathered around,
Hear the chanting sound,
'Double, double toil and trouble,
Fire burn and cauldron bubble'.

Adding in the bat's eye, like a moon in the sky,
With a hint of apple pie,
And salt and pickled pepper,
Plus a bickering bird's feather.

A pinch of dust,
This spell must
Have an eagle's wing,
Can you hear all the witches sing?

A dab of this,
A hint of that,
Lastly a cute cat's tail,
Now this special spell should never fail.

Hear the bubbling sound,
Fire darting all around,
Hear the cackling witches cry,
'Now you must die!'

Hayley Pemble (13)
King Ethelbert School, Birchington

The New Boy Poem

My first day at King Ethelbert
I put on my new trousers and shirt
Then my first day's journey had begun

Mrs Ruston was at the gate to welcome everyone
When I arrived at school I worried
To the hall I hurried, I had to find a seat
Ready for new people I would meet
Ms Rossiter is helpful and fun
She is 7G's tutor, number 1
She teaches us number work
When I finish I look back and smirk

I learn science, English and art
These things are taught to make me smart
I like science the best
Because it is better than all the rest

I eat lunch in the canteen
Where I sit it is so clean
The food there tastes great
So I make sure I'm not late

In geography I learn to read a map
And I listen to girls yap
In most of my lessons I have fun
But science is still the best one

When the day ends I leave school with my friends
We talk about our day
Sometimes I wish we could stay.

Andrew Lucas (12)
King Ethelbert School, Birchington

My Mum

My mum Janette is a fabulous mum,
She is the best mum in the world,
She's always there when I need a hand,
She's loving and caring,
Although we have had some bad moments,
She's always close to my heart.

She has loved me since I was small,
And I have loved her back,
She has cared for my brother and me,
No matter what's wrong,
She teaches me most of the things I know,
She's always close to my heart.

When I was small she cared for me,
When I was ill she was there for me,
She has always sat me on her knee,
She buys me cool clothes and treats,
She gets me great birthday prezzies,
She's always close to my heart.

She helps me when I need help,
She even helps me with my homework,
She makes me dinner, lunch and breakfast,
She's there for me 24/7,
I love her more than the world,
She's always close to my heart.

She's the person I know the most,
She cares for me,
And her patients at the hospital,
And my dad and brother,
She's always been close to my heart.

Gemma Peverett (12)
King Ethelbert School, Birchington

My Mum

My mum Sue is the best mum in the world,
She helps me out when I need help,
She makes me laugh,
And she's always there when I need her the most,
My mum is the best.

My mum Sue is the best mum in the world
She buys me the greatest things
And takes me out to the most amazing places,
My mum is the best.

My mum was always there when I was ill,
She has always been there when my brother was ill,
She was there when my sister was ill,
My mum's the greatest.

My mum has cared for me all my life,
She's the person I know the best,
Mums should be there 24/7
And she always has been,
My mum's perfect.

My mum has loved me all my life,
And I've loved her back,
She's a loving and generous mum,
No other mum could beat my mum.

Her heart must be huge,
All the love she has in it must be tight inside,
She hugs and kisses me but I pull away,
But inside I still love her very, very much,
She's always close to my heart,
She's the perfect mum,
I love her.

Amy Heath (12)
King Ethelbert School, Birchington

Double! Double!

(Based on 'Macbeth')

'Double, double toil and trouble'
Whisker of a rat, a big bee sting
Rabbit's leg, a seagull's wing
'Double, double toil and trouble'
A sharp tooth of a shark
Which was taken in the dark
'Double, double toil and trouble'
A silvery saliva of a snail
Bulldog's wagging tail
Like a Hell broth boil and bubble
'Double, double toil and trouble'
Fur of a ginger cat
An eye of a bat
'Double, double toil and trouble.'

Lois Hetterley (14)
King Ethelbert School, Birchington

Spell Poem

(Based on 'Macbeth')

On a hill, three witches meet
With nothing but dirt covering their feet
On the floor, near the door
There's some dead animal or something more

'Double, double toil and trouble'
The witches chant amongst the rubble
In a cauldron, in the middle
They chuck in some mice's dribble

Round, round in the pot
The whole thing smelling of rot
Maybe it is, or maybe it's not
In goes the cat's snot.

Matthew Ayling (14)
King Ethelbert School, Birchington

Witches' Warning Spell

(Based on 'Macbeth')

In a pot goes the best,
Eye of newt and toe of frog,
Wool of sheep and tooth of dog,
With bark from a log,
All around the cauldron black.

'Double, double toil and trouble,
Fire burn and cauldron bubble'.

From the sack the witch pulls out,
The ear of a mad monkey,
The lock to a gold key,
The witches are excited for thee,
Whoever decides to drink.

'Double, double toil and trouble,
Fire burn and cauldron bubble'.

The whiff from the mixture,
Is like a smell from Hell.
Thick, green and bubbling,
Will the spell work?

'Double, double toil and trouble,
Fire burn and cauldron bubble'.

Sinead Hallett (14)
King Ethelbert School, Birchington

Spell Poem

(Inspired by 'Macbeth')

A cave to the north on the moor.
A place where birds fear to soar.

Three witches sit and think.
They're thinking, *Who should drink?*

Their cauldron bubbling hot.
Their ingredients fail for nought.

A dash of blood from goats.
The Devil's wheats and oats.

A live, wriggling bat.
Could we do without that?

A touch of dragon foul smell.
It's like the stench of Hell.

Some mouldy ear of cat.
The tail and nose of rat.

King Duncan's bloody beard.
Man, they were pretty weird.

Banquo's mighty blade.
Of course, he was still slayed!

Joshua Mincher (14)
King Ethelbert School, Birchington

Pet Animals

Cats scratch
Dogs bite
Rabbits bite with all their might
Snails crawl
Dogs drawl
Spiders climb up the wall

Cats love mice
Dogs love bones
Rabbits love carrots
Snails love leaves
And spiders love flies

Cats will cuddle
Dogs will jump
Rabbits will hop
Snails will pop
And spiders will climb

But best of all pets
Is a swimming
Bubble-blowing
Fish!

Jade Dugggan (11)
King Ethelbert School, Birchington

3 Witches

(Based on 'Macbeth')

'Double, double toil and trouble
Fire burn and cauldron bubble.'

Beak of eagle, claw of cat
Toe of newt, gut of rat.

In the cauldron boil and bake
Whole of coiled snake.

Nail of toe, bark of tree
What about a sting of bee?

Tooth of canine, tooth of shark
Tooth of wolf in the dark.

Slime of slug and juice of bug
Dust from a couture rug.

Like a dragon, fierce and strong
The cauldron bubbles all night long.

Tamara Joyce (13)
King Ethelbert School, Birchington

The Furious Dragon

Zooming through the air the dragon flew like a gust of wind
Eyes like piercing red laser beams
Its shiny gold scales shone as the sun glowed on him
The head looked like a bomb but felt like a heavy rock
Claws were like swords ready for a prey to catch
Tail like an enormous arrow
Wings like massive fans coloured red like flames
The dragon's breath was like rotten eggs
He smelt like blood and looked like it too.

Marina Qattan (11)
Longford Community School, Feltham

The Dragon

Sleeping softly on the rocks the dragon snores loudly,
Eyes piercing red like rubies in the light,
As day dawned the dragon became more camouflaged
Like a chameleon on a branch,
Breath like the shimmering sun,
More men came and died by the head like an arrow,
The more it flew the more the spiky legs got sharper
Like a knife,
The fierce body, the shape of a helicopter,
Was more round like a circle.
Its wings are colossal, ribbed like a bat,
Tail whipping the rocks in the night,
The dragon's movement fast like a cheetah,
As the scales gleamed in the light it flew higher and higher.

Emma O'Brien (11)
Longford Community School, Feltham

Butterfly

Flying through the sky above me was a butterfly, it crossed me
Its beautiful body colour shines in the sunlight like a flash
It flew to each flower digging its head into the anther
Sucking the life out of the flowers
It got closer and closer, my eyes went blurry
It was like the butterfly kissed me
It felt like an angel had awoken me
I didn't even want to breathe in case I scared it away
My face went purple because I wasn't breathing for so long
The butterfly mistook me for a flower
And settled on my face
I sneezed and it flew away into the sun.

Hayley Elliott (12)
Longford Community School, Feltham

Environment

We cut down trees,
Thinking we're doing no harm.
But we're wrong.
Where do birds live?
In the trees.
What about monkeys?
In the trees.
When we cut down trees,
We're destroying their homes.

When we cover fields
With cement and concrete,
We're blocking up mole holes
So they're trapped underneath.
We're destroying homes to many creatures,
We're destroying feeding grounds
Especially when we build towns.
Do something before the animals are all gone!

Carly Parker (12)
Longford Community School, Feltham

The Lion With The Metal Body

See the car big and strong
Roaring as it goes
Eyes shining in the dark
Breathing through its nose
Four feet pounding on the ground
Trying not to make a sound
Twisting, turning, a bumpy sensation
Finally getting to its destination.

The lion with the metal body.

Emily Gates (12)
Longford Community School, Feltham

Tsunami Disaster

T he air is filled with death and fear
S o many families lost their dear
U nder the rubble bodies rot
N ow there's a dirty and tarred up cot
A s a baby struggles in hospital
M any houses destroyed, now nothing at all
I 'm in despair to see all this

D ead people burnt, I don't know how
I s this the end of paradise?
S till nothing's left, not even some mice
A s dead one's families cry as hummingbirds hum
S urviving on the aids that come
T ens of thousands live in fear
E ver waiting for help to hear
R ed with blood in hospital, they need your aid for years to come.

Please help the tsunami disaster any way you can
And help save lives today!

Lana Louise Watters (11)
Longford Community School, Feltham

Corkscrew

The giant elephant pulls the brown wood with its long, steel tusks
Watch and oversee as the wood's lifted
Then watch as the wood gets scarred
Now get ready for the big bang
And *thizz* and *thizz* of the surprise inside
The giant elephant then rests.

Lewis Metcalfe (12)
Longford Community School, Feltham

Death's Fruit

Lifeless
Shrouded in darkness and mystery
Shadows seeping
To form hollow blotches on its skin

Harmless
Or so it may seem at first
Isolated and solitary
Motionless and yet drawing nearer

Meaningless
To the closed mind
The curved blade
Of the cloaked man's scythe

Sadness
The core of its symbolism
Black spots
Contrasted by a dying yellow.

Bryan Dollery (15)
Longford Community School, Feltham

Lawnmower

The lawnmower is deadly,
It has very long tongs,
To eat the grass stand by stand.
As you press the button,
It chomps and clatters,
And finally devours the grass.

So be careful when you turn on the lawn mower,
Because a lawnmower is always hungry,
For more than just grass!

And when the grass is shorter than short,
The hungry lawnmower,
Has finished his mission.

Jade Stroudley (12)
Longford Community School, Feltham

Eagle

He flies through the sky
Soaring through the clouds as he goes by,
The cold wind makes him go numb
But he still seems to carry on by.

When he reaches his hill and crouches down
No one knows why,
He digs his beak into the soft, fertile ground
And it looks like he is sniffing around.

He lifts off the ground
But this time with something in his grasp,
It's a very small creature, smaller than him.
We think it's a rabbit, good enough for lunch.
He lands on a tree to eat his prey
But takes little bites and gives it to what looks like his young.

As he leaves off again, we don't know why,
When we climbed up the tree
We wanted to cry,
As we saw them there tight,
The sun came out big and bright.

They started to wake, whinged out loud,
And before we knew it
We were on the ground,
Being attacked by something proud,
So we ran with another crowd.

Rhys William Last (12)
Longford Community School, Feltham

A Washing Machine

Watch the washing machine chew up all your clothes
With its spinning wheel and see your washing getting gobbled up.
The noise sounds like a roaring car with the engine playing
And watch it eat its prey all up.

Adam Fowler (12)
Longford Community School, Feltham

This Room

This room, a soft pink and red
The hearts surrounding me in passion and warmth
My heart filling with love and romance
A four-poster bed that has frilly covers
Just like a little baby's dress.

The smell of candy sweets, refreshing my nose
My mouth watering as the cleanliness hits my tongue
Pure white doves whistling happily
Outside on the bright green trees
My body calm and peace around me.

A young woman stood
By a pure white dressing table
In a dress so long and elegant
It is her special day
Her wedding day
Her face filled with delight
Her soft voice whispers,
'Please take a photo.'

The dressing table
Smooth and tender
Glaring at the bride
With intensity, just waiting
For that time to arrive.

Samantha Baldwin (15)
Longford Community School, Feltham

Waves

The waves came out to play today
They swirl, they crash, they twirl
They hiss, they whoosh, they spit
They trap you on an island
Where no one is around
The waves came out to play today
I wish, I wish, I wish.

Billie Stephana Brockway (12)
Longford Community School, Feltham

Gone

As I saw the trickle
    Of his tears,
My heart sank,
    I knew she was gone,
Gone for good.

Her smile was sweet,
    Like a ripe orange's juice.
Her skin was smooth,
    Like an orange's peel.
But she was gone,
    Gone for good.

She was like a chair,
    Sitting in a dark, dark room
Waiting to be sat on,
    Or just to have company.
But she is gone,
    Gone for good.

She was like an orange,
    Fresh, sweet and bright,
But she was gone,
    Gone forever.

Wendy-Hannah May (14)
Longford Community School, Feltham

Headache Poem

This headache of mine, it's driving me mad,
I've had it so long, it's making me sad.
My head is swirling, whirling and turning,
It's making my eyes start burning.
I wanted it to stop,
I made it worse, I gave it a bop.
Spinning, spinning all around,
It's making me fall on the ground.
Striking out the pain till it happens again.

Jack Johnson (12)
Longford Community School, Feltham

Chocolate Cake

A spongy chocolate cake
Is as scrumptious
As anything that you can eat

When it is freshly baked
The chocolate drips down endlessly
To the bottom of the cake

If you take a big bite
You sink your teeth
Until you rip it off

It all drips down your mouth
And it's all over it
You lick your lips and take another bite
This time a gigantic bite

Take another and another
The cake slides down your throat
Slowly, slooowly.

Bhavina Vadgama (12)
Longford Community School, Feltham

I Wrote Your Name

I wrote your name in the sand
But the sea washed it away.

I wrote your name in the sky
But the wind blew it away.

I wrote your name in my heart
And forever it will stay.

Jessica Bellfield (12)
Longford Community School, Feltham

Important Things!

Some families have relatives that are
Big or small,
Short or tall,
Fat or thin,
Maybe even bony or possibly dead.

People also have pets that are
Black or white,
Dark or bright,
Poodles can be purple or pink,
Some animals are fresh or stink.

Friends are also important, they are
Smart or dumb,
Boring or fun,
Happy or sad,
Calm or mad.

Family, friends and also pets
Are very important to you,
They make you happy,
They are there to support you!

These are the important things in life!

Chantel Faye Dyte (11)
Longford Community School, Feltham

Toaster

Hard tummy with boiling flames,
Slowly cooking its toasty victims,
The victims start to burn,
Then suddenly it stops and shoots them into the air,
They land on a plate for a crispy crunch in your . . .
Toast.

Kathryn Evans (11)
Longford Community School, Feltham

What Is This Place?

Swirling emotions run riot,
Bouncing off the four walls around me,
A crimson mist lurks around my feet,
There's a low humming sound like a bee.

Towering smiles and full thought memories,
Go whizzing, racing past my view,
I watch this tiny world grow behind these four walls,
The things I see are old and new.

A sweetish smell fills the air,
There is a world within this room,
And within this world there is only love,
No pain, no death, no gloom.

I do not feel imprisoned,
As I stand in the corner of this tiny space,
A pink glow lights up the room,
This is mine, this is a safe place.

I wonder where I am,
I don't know if I really care,
I don't know what this room is,
But I know that I'm meant to be there.

I think the images I'm seeing,
Are the pieces of my life, each part,
I think this room is my soul,
I think this room is my heart.

Rachel Twohey (15)
Longford Community School, Feltham

Manchester United

M an United
A lways winning
N ever loses
C heering for the
H ome team
E nds the game with
S miles and
T ears
E veryone clapping
R unning the team

U nited playing
N eck and neck
I n the stand
T ill the sun goes down
E nds the season till
D eath comes to all.

Charles Byrne (11)
Longford Community School, Feltham

I'm Thinking Of You

You came into my life sent down from Heaven
I'm thinking of you 24/7.

You are always there for me even when I'm sad
Living without you would make me go mad.

When you are not around I'm always blue
You just have to remember I will always be thinking of you.

I love you, I hope we will never be apart
You, my love, have now got my heart.

You will always be mine for now and forever
You will always be mine for you are my treasure.

You will always be, please tell me it's true
Please be mine, I will always love you.

Lauren Woods (11)
Longford Community School, Feltham

Like A Sun In A View

This is for my uncle who has died.
I love you, I love you.
You're warm and cuddly
And you will be there for me.

I love you, I love you like a sun in a view.
My love for you will go on and on
Just for you.

I will miss hearing you shout,
I will miss hearing you talk
And the most I will miss you.

Amelia Mullen (12)
Longford Community School, Feltham

The Best Place To Be

The sea, the sunset, the waves, the beach,
A more calming place is out of reach,
Relaxing, peaceful, graceful, tranquil,
Along the beach is the best place to chill.

With the waves swirling in-between my toes,
Around my ankles, soaking my clothes,
Waves lapping against overhanging cliffs,
The sea possesses its own genuine gift.

Empty and solitary, nobody around,
Apart from the odd thin and wispy cloud,
All I can smell is the salt from the sea,
As well as the food scents from across the street.

But regardless of this,
The beach and the sea,
Above anything else,
It's the best place to be.

Georgie Giddings (14)
Longford Community School, Feltham

This Room

As I close my eyes,
I see deep, dark colours,
Red and purple.
Somewhere exotic.
I smell incense,
It's strong and suffocating.

In the distance I see a room,
The atmosphere is quiet, relaxing.
Calming music piped all around.
I feel I want to meditate,
And wash my worries away.

A bed overflowing with drapes,
By the window,
Seems to be breathing slowly.
It's listening with me,
I'm not alone.
We have escaped,
Even if only for a moment.

Laura Cripps (15)
Longford Community School, Feltham

Sea Life

The sea is cool and calm
Let's go deep down
Down through the wavy seaweed
As it brushes against your face
Go down, down
Let's swim through the rocks
And bump your way
Push the rough sea outta your way
To find a . . . *shark!*
So swim, swim down
Down to find yourself with your mates
Let's swim, swim away from this place.

Amie Boardman (12)
Longford Community School, Feltham

Inside My Head

I'm in a room,
A grey room.
I'm bored because of my loneliness,
I'm surrounded by cobwebs.
I try to open the single window,
I choke on the dust that smothers it.
It smothered the window like fire on a burning wall.

I can taste the damp that seeps through the walls.
The droning sound of my shallow breathing,
Makes the cobwebs shiver.
A tear falls onto my cheek,
I try to cry out the boredom.
But . . .
I'm too drained to move.

Thomas Mutton
Longford Community School, Feltham

A Dark Day

The sky is dark and grey.
I wonder what will happen today?
I went down the park, saw a dog bark
And ran away.

I went around Tom's.
He pinched me with tongs.
I started to cry
And turned away.

I went back home,
Fell into a deep sleep.
Nobody made a peep.
It was a dark day.

Matthew Lewis (11)
Longford Community School, Feltham

Emotions About Peace

Why is this world not peaceful?
Why is this world filled with crime?
Why do death events have to happen?
This is what I will never get.

Why is this world filled with sloth and anger?
Why has this world got wars?
Why do people do something wrong
Then they try to do something wrong again?
This is what I will never get.

Why do friends have to split up?
Why does this world have to have mafia?
Why do people have to blackmail to just get what they want?
This is what I will never get.

Why do people solve things with anger?
Why do people have to kill and do not even care?
Why do people have to be racist to a person that is Muslim,
Jewish or Hindu?
Why do people have to be racist at all?
This is what I will never ever get.

Milad Kazava Keshvari (11)
Longford Community School, Feltham

Boy And Girl

Boys, boys
Who play with their toys
Boys, boys
Who make lots of noise!
Girls, girls
Who like to play with their curls
Girls, girls
Who like their pearls.

Carla Burlow (12)
Longford Community School, Feltham

A Monster In My Bedroom

'There's a monster in my bedroom, Mum,
I think his name is Ben.
He's purple, red, yellow, blue,
And I think his name is Ben.

There's a monster in my bedroom, Mum,
Run, Mum, run, run, run,
Down the stairs, out the door,
Quick, he's eaten my bun!

There's a monster in my bedroom, Mum,
Oh no! He's blocked the door!
Quick, Mum, phone Dad,
Need more food, more, more, more!

There's a monster in my bedroom, Mum,
Dad's now got the gun,
He's shot him. *Yes!* We've won!'
And that's the end of my tale!

Hannah Roche (11)
Longford Community School, Feltham

Friendship!

F riendship means you should be
R esponsible. Sometimes it can be
I ncredible. Having a best friend is
E specially great. You must be
N ice to each other. You are
D ifferent from each other but you keep
S ecrets. You are
H appy together. You must have
I ntelligence to keep a best friend. The best times are
P eaceful and contain no anger.

Stephanie Christine Franklin (12)
Longford Community School, Feltham

The Way She Was

She stands happily laughing, her hair blonde and long
The radio in her bedroom plays her favourite song
She sings into her hairbrush, just like microphone
Her friends dance beside her, she never was alone
Her skirt and T-shirt tight, how the pop stars used to wear
She loved how people would look and smile
And always stop and stare
She loved to be noticed and seen at every place
She would always smile even though she hated her brace
She was always the one who was first to do everything
To come up with an idea or to show a dance or sing
Her homework would always suffer and of all things came last
She'd rather enjoy hanging out with her friends
And having a blast.

For that was the old her that she left behind
To take responsibility and get things in on time
For now her life has changed for better and for worse
She has less time for fun but more money in her purse
She left her dreams of fame behind to dreams of house and home
There is no more singing into a hairbrush microphone
She still has that smile as there's so much she's grateful for
Children that love her and a husband that she adores
I stare at the picture of how she used to be
At a time of no responsibility, a time without my sis and me
I sometimes stare at the picture and I smile because
I see the way I am in the way she was.

Amy Castle (15)
Longford Community School, Feltham

The World

The bluebirds lay in the meadow
The ponies graze on the hill
The sun is rising from the Earth
And the world is waking again

The cows lay in the sun
The blackbirds make their summer nests
The sun is rising from the Earth
And the world is waking again

The children run out from school
The parents hug and kiss
The sun is rising from the Earth
And the world is waking again

The moon is falling quicker now
The daytime stays longer
The sun is rising from the Earth
And the world is waking again

The workers work all day
The children start to play
The sun is rising from the Earth
And the world is waking again

The school is ending at the same time
The day is lasting longer
The sun is rising from the Earth
And the world is waking again

The bluebirds lay in the meadow
The ponies graze on the hills
The sun is rising from the Earth
And the world is waking again.

Jack Twohey (12)
Longford Community School, Feltham

The Dead Town

The hungry birds call stubbornly
All you can hear is the scramble,
Of brambles struggling to wake
The dead town up.

There's nobody responding,
But there's this clock still ticking,
And there's this river with fresh water.

I waited with an emissary's patience,
Maybe they ran away from the doom-surge-haunted lights.

All I could do was ride off on my fast-galloping horse quietly
And leave the town in its intricate and astonishing way.

Millicent Mukombe (15)
Longford Community School, Feltham

Gymnastics

I'm sitting in my auntie's car,
Hope it's not too far.
Another competition,
I'm going to win, win, win.

I'm sitting in the changing room,
I've got butterflies in my tummy.
There's an hour left till I am on,
Why don't I have something scrummy?

In my competition,
I'm going to win, win, win.

I have done my competition,
It was fun.
I was very good,
'Cause I have won.

Natasha Drury (11)
Longford Community School, Feltham

My Dragon

Flying through the air
The dragon zoomed through the clouds
Eyes like red flames

Shiny silver scales shimmered as the sun shone on him
Claws sharp as a dozen razors all put together
Grasping his prey to eat

Tail swooping left to right, over and over again
Wings were as big as a giant's foot
With all the colours of a rainbow

The dragon's skin was really thick so he didn't get hurt
His breath was like a stinky onion
That nearly made me faint.

Emily Davies (11)
Longford Community School, Feltham

My Hobbies, Horses

H orses are my hobby
O h what fun they are
B ouncing on their little backs
B eing around them all
I go and see them at the weekend
E arly in the morning
S eeing them makes me happy, I really love them all

H orses are my favourite
O h I love them lots
R iding in the green grass fields
S eeing them enjoying themselves
E asily getting scared
S teadying them again.

Amber Chapman (11)
Longford Community School, Feltham

Manchester United

M atchball has been kicked,
A lex Ferguson set out the team he picked,
N ever lost a game this season,
C helsea want to end that for a reason,
H orrified fans watched the football,
E ngland's defender looking cool,
S mithy came close for Saha to tap in,
T he United fans were sure it was a win,
E xcited Fergie cheered,
R uud van Nistelrooy did the same.

U nited players left the field,
N eville knew the title was sealed,
I n the changing rooms the champagne came out,
T hen Chelsea went home with nowt,
E nd of the season United won,
D evastated Chelsea and Arsenal went home none.

Ryan Foskett (11)
Longford Community School, Feltham

Ice-Cold Dragon

Skidding along the ice
Trying to catch his prey,
He thinks it's time to get his revenge
For another day.
So angry his colours change into a dark red,
Gliding along, in and out the ice rocks,
Eyes flickering left and right,
Concentrating so hard his scales start to shiver!
Spider-webbed wings blowing in the snow,
People shooting arrows,
But he can't die
Unless you shoot an arrow with holy water through his heart!

Chloé Shaw (11)
Longford Community School, Feltham

Manchester United

M an U ready to play
A ll the players lined up
N ew kits are ready
C rowds are cheering
H orror between the teams
E nd of waiting
S tart the match
T hey've scored, it's Scholes!
E qualiser by Arsenal, it's Henry!
R ef blows for half-time.

U nited are ready for the second half
N ow it's Giggs' turn to score the goal!
I 've never seen such a great game
T he crowd are going wild
E du has scored for Arsenal
D raw! What a game!

Thomas Smith (11)
Longford Community School, Feltham

Love Is A Strange Thing

Every time that person walks in the room,
I feel as if a flower is about to bloom,
And that makes me scared 'cause he might be my groom.
Love is a strange thing.

My heart starts to fly every time he walks by,
Every time he walks by I am up in the sky,
Somebody help me, I'm getting quite high.
Love is a strange thing.

Every time he touches me a shiver runs up my spine,
I was on the phone to him until half-past nine,
I'm so shaky but I thought I was fine.
Love is a strange thing.

Demi Louise Gilham (11)
Longford Community School, Feltham

A Night On The Town

As she leaves her room and walks down the stairs
I look, gasp and stare.
I've never seen that piece before.
She hid this until we needed to know
This strange, beautiful side of her.
It's so unlike the figure I'm used to seeing,
The mother who worked unlike anything else I'd seen.
The pink leather miniskirt made its debut today
As she hits a night on the town
As an independent, single woman.

Thomas Mutton (15)
Longford Community School, Feltham

Feelings And Emotions

Feeling a bit low,
Sad and upset.
I feel all alone, no one by my side.
Lonely and thinking about things.
Things like friends and family.
I am sitting in my bedroom all alone,
Thinking, thinking . . .

Amy Morris (12)
Longford Community School, Feltham

The Tsunami

T sunami hit my country bad
S creaming and shouting is all I heard
U nhappy people crying
N o one thought of smiling
A dmiration is what I have got
M any people haven't got a lot
 I n my eyes I'm lucky to be alive.

Jodie Longuehaye (11)
Longford Community School, Feltham

The Long Walk Home

(Inspired by the film 'The Long Walk Home')

Some time ago in London a group of small people arrived,
Then all of a sudden they were taken for granted
By the people who would not give a ride.
White men shall not rest till the black people are dead
Till all of them are gone, the white man shall not rest.
In the end the white men gave lots and lots of freedom
After a lifetime's fight.

Sam Young (11)
Longford Community School, Feltham

The Tsunami

T he tsunami brings pain and tears
S ends water up the shore
U nder the water bodies lay
N o way to survive
A sia has been affected too
M ums and dads have lost their kids
 I n the tsunami.

Ashley Jaggi (11)
Longford Community School, Feltham

Chelsea

C helsea is the best
H ip hip hooray
E veryone supports them
L ampard is the key
S tamford Bridge is home
E veryone supports us
A t Chelsea Football Club.

John Wood (11)
Longford Community School, Feltham

The Battle Of Terror

Soldiers walked by like a band
And all the women started to cry,
They shoved a gun in my hand
And told me to fight or die.

Now I stand in a trench
Like a kid standing behind a fence,
The men start crying,
The bodies start dying.

Now we go home,
We still haven't grown,
And now I feel so alone.

Glenn Stevens (12)
Oakwood School, Bexleyheath

Never Come Back
And Greet Me With Your Smile

Never come back and greet me with your smile,
I know that smile of yours is just a lie.
I wish it would just leave me for a while,
But thinking of you makes me want to cry.

Each thorn on every rose you gave me,
They are like knives stabbing into my heart.
Now you're gone I can once again be free,
Each laugh of yours was like a poison dart.

Never will I forgive what you have done,
You've destroyed my life now I cannot live.
My love for you is now a burning sun,
My love for you has drained out through a sieve.

I thought we would be as one together,
But that memory has gone forever.

Emily Cunningham & Tiffany Soule (13)
St Antony's Leweston School, Sherborne

Shall I Compare Thee To A Microwave?

(Based on 'Sonnet 18' by William Shakespeare)

Shall I compare thee to a microwave?
Thou art more powerful, more temperate.
Sharp forks do pierce the darling spuds from Dave
Although his love had all too short a date.
Sometimes too hot the twirly pasta boils,
And often on our plates does it remain.
And every other chicken dish I spoil,
Which means the gravy ends up down the drain.
But now your wondrous cooking shall not fade,
Nor will the sausages be undercooked.
So ne'er again will flour be misweighed.
My darling chef, you know you have me hooked!
So long as you can cook, and cook for me,
So long cooks this, and this bakes cakes for thee!

Harriet Nelham Clark, Rosanna Radford & Zoë Tweedie (14)
St Antony's Leweston School, Sherborne

Ways Of Nature

Elephant, your trunk is nature's sword,
Gentle giant
Lion, your mane is an eiderdown quilt,
Fearsome hunger
Rhino, your horns are made from dust of moon,
Creature of power,
Leopard, your fur, run over by a million ducks,
Night crawler
Eagle, your eyes are glass beads,
Flying death trap,
Flamingo, your neck is a silken scarf,
Pink fluff ball.

Human, your hands ruin all . . .

Kate Bridgeman-Sutton (12)
St Antony's Leweston School, Sherborne

The Caterpillar's Life

Heart beating faster,
Urging herself
Forwards,
But she is slow
And wings are fast.
It's a million to one
That she will
Last.
But still she squirms,
Now she can feel
Its claws burn.
Her ugly skin
Shivers within.
Bang
Yet what is this?
Could it be
That gruesome bird
Will never
Be true to his word?
As now he falls,
Down and down,
Though he has gone,
She will never be found.
Down and down,
Nearer and nearer,
She utters a silent scream,
That will never be heard.
And then . . .
Splat!

Louise Newton (12)
St Antony's Leweston School, Sherborne

Triolet

Too long have I lain awake
All alone
The cold is piercing, making me shake
Too long have I lain awake
My expression an icy lake
The skin on my fingers hangs down from the bone
Too long have I lain awake
All alone . . .

Madeleine Love (13)
St Antony's Leweston School, Sherborne

You Remind Me Of A Thorn

You remind me of a thorn
That sticks into my side.
I've felt it since you were born,
You remind me of a thorn.
For you my love has died.
You remind me of a thorn
That sticks into my side.

Charlotte Robinson (14)
St Antony's Leweston School, Sherborne

Sad And Depressed

Sad and depressed
Wanting a cruise
Crumbled and messed
Sad and depressed
Run out of zest
Thinking of booze
Sad and depressed
Wanting a cruise.

Aurora Moxon (13)
St Antony's Leweston School, Sherborne

Hazel

(This poem is dedicated to the memory of Hazel who was my best friend)

A girl I always looked up to
And a girl everyone else did too.

She bounded around,
Made a daisy chain crown,
With her flowing blonde hair twisted round.

I looked in her eyes and saw friendship,
It was a shame it didn't last.

When her heart pulled the plug
I never could shrug.

I could never have a best friend again!

Tabitha Nelham Clark (12)
St Antony's Leweston School, Sherborne

Daydreamer

Unaware of life, death is near
Thinking about another world
Vacant expressions, shows no feeling
Startled back to reality, pain
Unaware of life, death is near.

Sophie Danby & Isabelle Barber (11)
St Antony's Leweston School, Sherborne

Daydreamer

Unaware of existent time
Thinking about creation
Vacant new eyes
Startled back to herself, reality
Unaware of existent time.

Emily Hewett (11)
St Antony's Leweston School, Sherborne

Bat

(This poem is dedicated to Neo, my trusty friend, pet and hot water bottle)

Waiting for the sun to set
In the dusk together they met.

Their eyes are open but nought they see
Ears are the guide away from the tree.

Swirling, whirling, criss-crossing in air
Each one has a unique flair.

Sweeping, swooping, snapping up prey
At every moth that enters the fray.

Then returning to the roost
Flying with an extra boost.

Before the black of the night fades
Before the sun's first light.

Sophie Tuppen (12)
St Antony's Leweston School, Sherborne

The Rabbits

Rabbits in a field
The owner does not yield
He shouts against the wind
He's a rabbit's hateful fiend
He disappears like a ghost
He's not the nicest host
You see a silent flash
But the rabbits do not dash
The wind cannot disguise
The fiend's hateful eyes
As a rabbit falls down dead
All the other rabbits fled.

Jennifer Ward (11)
St Antony's Leweston School, Sherborne

A Lonely Valentine's Rhyme

I need no valentine,
Nor chocolates or a rose.
For no charming youth I pine,
I need no valentine,
No love to hold for all of time.
It's this day I loath,
I need no valentine,
Nor chocolates or a rose.

Sofia Marsaglia (13)
St Antony's Leweston School, Sherborne

If This Day Was My Last

If this day was my last
I would spend it with you.
I would forget the past
If this day was my last.
Life passes so fast
Even with hours so few.
If this day was my last
I would spend it with you.

Bryony Edwards (13)
St Antony's Leweston School, Sherborne

The Horses

Horses gallop over grassy plains.
Bucking and rearing and running wild.
Swift over the ground they glide.
Manes and tails flying behind.
Until we meet again, my friends.
You will gallop the grassy plains.

Daisy Crichton (11)
St Antony's Leweston School, Sherborne

Things To Do With A Newspaper

I love to be a paper
You can use me for fire
I come in different colours
You can make books with me
You can wrap your fish and chips in me
You can put me on a wall and draw pictures on me
Make a hat
Decorate a room
You can write a message
You can read me
I love to be written on
You can cut me up
People live in me, animals use me to clear mess up
I can be ripped, screwed up and put in the bin
Which I don't like
I come from a tree
And would like to be there now.

Sarah Isaac (14)
St Anthony's School, Margate

The Starry Night

It was a starry night,
Where the hills were bright
And there was a kite
On this quiet night.
There was a mighty fight
With a strong knight
Which ended in a flash of light.

George Nash (14)
St Anthony's School, Margate

What Can You Do With A Ruler?

I love being a ruler
People draw lines with me
Sometimes I hate to be a rule
Because people smash me on the desk
People measure in centimetres
I feel happy sometimes
Some people twang me and I don't like it
People use me to cut paper
People snap me
People ping me all the time
People build things with me
People hurt other people with me
Some people like me
Some people lick me on the head
This is disgusting
I want to be used
To measure and draw with.

Judith Bryant (14)
St Anthony's School, Margate

The Dog

I have a dog who likes to sniff
Who slinks around bins looking for bones
In parks he likes to race and pounce
Wagging his tail with pleasure
He loves to crouch and then stretch
He rolls on his back for a tickle.

Christian Sawyer (15)
St Anthony's School, Margate

The Whale

It moves very slowly
And gracefully in the water
It dives up and down
Using its tail to splash
Water blows out of its head
Exploding into the air
When it wants food
It opens its mouth very wide
All the little fishes go inside
It dives very deep
Holding its breath
Then exploding to the surface
The baby whale swims very close
Mum is protecting it
Sometimes they touch.

Danielle Barlow (14), Toni Edwards & Stephanie Burdge (15)
St Anthony's School, Margate

Hamsters

They race on their wheel for half of the day,
Climb up the cage looking for an escape.
They sleep all night and roll in the corner,
They twitch their noses,
And they wriggle their ears,
Getting up for something to eat.

Paul Moore (14)
St Anthony's School, Margate

Dolphin Movements

The dolphin protects people
It saves them from sharks.
It swims around them
Whacks it with its flipper.

The dolphin follows a ship
It jumps in and out.
It rides the waves
Up and over it goes.

The dolphin's in a show
It jumps through a hoop.
It flips in the air
And turns a somersault.

The dolphin in the wild
Is very intelligent.
It has good hearing
And is very strong.

The dolphin opens its mouth
To get close to food.
It sounds like it's laughing
Or squeaking to say hello.

Robert Beith (15)
St Anthony's School, Margate

Dundee Man

There was an old man from Dundee,
Who had a big, gold front door key.
He opened a door,
Couldn't believe what he saw.
It was huge, great, stormy, blue sea.

Fiona Hodges (15)
St Anthony's School, Margate

Recycling

I am a newspaper.
I have led a good life.
Now to be recycled.
Thrown in a bin.
I get all dirty.
Water poured all over me.
I get very wet.
I am dissolving very fast.
All mushed up to a pulp.
Now I am dried in an oven.
Bleached with a liquid
And rolled into a drum.
Now I can be used again.
Ready to be written on.

Jamie Littlechild (14)
St Anthony's School, Margate

Cat Feature

The cat wants to play
It springs in the air
It climbs up the chair
And jumps everywhere

The cat wants to sleep
It is lazy and yawns
It starts to twitch
As it curls into a ball

The cat wants to eat
It goes to its bowl
It chews and swallows

The cat wants to hunt
It starts to stalk its prey
It creeps up to it
Then pounces in one leap.

Marc Foster (14)
St Anthony's School, Margate

Winter Haikus

Snow, ice, frost and mist
All join in together now
To make England freeze.

Children come to play
Brand new creatures to be found
Big, white, fat and round.

Snowflakes make me smile
So full of intricacy
Falling to the ground.

Zahra Tarjomani (14)
St Lawrence College, Ramsgate

Snowballs Haikus

Snow is so snowy
As snowy as snow can be
Snow is falling here.

Snow is white and cold
It falls on all things it sees
Snow falls everywhere.

Snow falls on the cars
Snow can travel everywhere
Snow falls on your head.

Christopher Allum (13)
St Lawrence College, Ramsgate

Snow - Haiku

It is so much fun,
You can't do it in the sun
Building a snowman.

Laura Shipley (11)
St Lawrence College, Ramsgate

Something Special

I can never find a present,
This reason is very true.
Because nothing I could find or buy,
Would show my love for you.

Flowers really aren't your thing,
And soft toys are forgotten.
Wine is not to your taste,
And fruit would end up rotten.

You prefer things that are different,
Creative, fun and clever.
So what better than a poem,
Stuck in your mind forever.

Created just for you.

Hannah Rebecca Mills (13)
St Lawrence College, Ramsgate

Winter!

As we watch the winter spread, thus covering the land,
He takes away our colours, our sun . . .
Till all is cold and bland!

As he leaves his icy trail for people there to find
All the joy and sunshine . . .
Have all been left behind.

He's replaced it all with sorrow, memories all but gone.
Vivid thoughts of summer and how her sun once shone.

Her sun did shine, her grass did grow, the joy that she did bring.
All consumed by winter now . . .
Her birds no longer sing.

His ice-cold grip is tightened now, memories fade away.
But for now the winter's here . . .
And here he's going to stay!

Luke Murphy (13)
St Michael's CE Middle School, Wimborne

Frost

Frost has descended and
Has stolen our colour.
Gone are the greens
Of the grass and the trees;
Gone is the colour of the cars
Beneath the blanket of Frost's breath.
Will warmth ever come?

Birds peck on their ice rink
Looking to drink;
Small mammals search for food
Beneath the concrete monster.
Trees stand like identical soldiers,
Frozen in time.
Will warmth ever come?

Inside, the cat looks on
With a smile on its face.
Street maps of ice corner the windows.
Frost has descended and
Stolen our time.
Will warmth ever come?

Slowly the sun rises
From its icy bed,
Casting fingers of warmth
To all but the shadows.
For now, Frost retreats from
The oncoming embrace,
Releasing our colours
And time.
Warmth has come.

Natalie Muncer (13)
St Michael's CE Middle School, Wimborne

Attack By The Marines

(Based on 'The Charge of the Light Brigade' by Alfred Lord Tennyson)

Half a harbour, half a harbour,
Half a harbour forward.
Through the death traps of the waves,
Travelled the eight hundred.
Sailing, sailing,
Charging to the island.
Onward to Brownsea Island,
Off the boat streamed the eight hundred.

Forward the marines,
There was no man afraid,
That the captain knew.
But there was something wrong,
Something that was an error.
Something that led to terror,
As they stood low.
Onward into the trap of death,
Ran the eight hundred.

Man with gun in front,
Man with gun behind,
Surrounded and threatened,
To and fro went the guns,
Shattered the gunshots.
Yet all fought with fear,
Not seen in their eyes.
Into the death trap,
Ran the eight hundred.

Megan Nutting (12)
St Michael's CE Middle School, Wimborne

The Platoon Of The Royal Marines

(Based on 'The Charge of the Light Brigade' by Alfred Lord Tennyson)

Two and half miles, two and half miles
Two and half miles to Brownsea Island
All towards the overtaken oil works
Charged the 96 soldiers.
'Forward, platoon!
Start the boat!' shouted the captain.
Into the overtaken oil works
Charged the 96 soldiers.

'Forward, platoon!'
Was there a man damned?
Not tho' the soldier knew
Someone had error'd
Theirs not to make reply,
Theirs not to reason why,
Theirs but to do or die:
Into the overtaken oil works
Charged the 96 soldiers.

Explosives to the right of them,
Explosives to the left of them,
Explosives in front of them,
Bangs and crashes.
Bombarded with flames and gunfire,
Trudged on with jeep and tyre,
Into the jaws of demise
Charged the 96 soldiers.

Flashed the guns bare,
Flashed the bullets in the air,
Shooting the terrorists there,
Stormed the platoon,
While the people wander'd,
Forced into the fiery mist.

They clashed with the terrorists,
Rebelling and radical activists,
Reel'd from the bullet's strike,
Crushed and bouldered
They ran back but not,
Not the 96 soldiers.

Explosives to the right of them,
Explosives to the left of them,
Explosives behind them,
Bangs and crashes.
Bombarded with flames and gunfire,
While mate and comrades desire,
That they have fought well.
Into the jaws of demise,
Back from the depths of Hell,
All that was remaining,
Remaining of the 96 soldiers.

When did their triumph fade?
O the wild charge they made!
All the people wonder'd
Honour the charge they plunder'd
Honour the platoon
Noble 96 soldiers!

Alex Richardson (13)
St Michael's CE Middle School, Wimborne

Black Ice

I'm a monster, thin and black,
I blend in with the flat tarmac.
You can't see me but I am there,
I can catch you unaware.
You'll slip, you'll skid, you'll slide all over,
Watch how I destroy this Rover.
Crash! Bang! Kablam! Wallop!

I'm like a soldier hiding out,
I've killed lots of people without a doubt.
I wait and wait for you to come by,
You'd better hope you do not die.
You'll slip, you'll skid, you'll slide all over,
Watch how I destroy that Rover.
Crash! Bang! Kablam! Wallop!

Now I'm sure the Rover's dead,
It's gone to Heaven to rest its head.
So be careful or you'll end up like him,
Dead! No spirit - just flesh and skin.
Some people say that I'm not nice,
What am I? I'm black ice.

Laura Payne (13)
St Michael's CE Middle School, Wimborne

Voice Of Cold

A blanket of snow, whiter than white,
Framed with the sharp and merciless ice,
Creeps a path from door to door,
Breaking boundaries, freezing more.
No human lingers for life has gone,
Emptiness where the sun once shone.
Frozen sculptures, carved to die,
Icicles freezing seconds in time.
Air so cold, one breath could kill,
Consumes all warmth and stands it still.
Dream becomes reality, it soon becomes clear,
Only frostbitten doom dwells here.

Joanna Corbet (12)
St Michael's CE Middle School, Wimborne

Sounds Good

Sausage sizzles,
Crisp bread cracks;
Hot dogs hiss
And flapjack snaps!

Bacon boils
And fritters fry;
Apples squelch
In apple pie.

Baked beans bubble,
Gravy grumbles;
Popcorn pops
And stomach rumbles . . .

I'm hungry!

Massah Sharka (11)
St Philomena's School, Carshalton

Sunflower

(Inspired by 'Daffodils' by William Wordsworth)

I am a little seed in the ground,
Where the cold, frosty snow
Shatters millions of snowflakes above me.
At the beginning of spring I maintain moisture,
I make a chance to break through my shell
And reach my small root down to the softest
Ground of dirt I can find.
Now I can just use my two leaves
And break out of my shell
And feel the ray of light shining above my bud.
Day by day, time after time
I grow so long, so tall,
I can be taller than a human being itself.
Now my face appears but still incomplete.
I still try to get stronger,
To get the sun shining on my face.
Finally my face shows itself
Above the sun and the sky which is so clear and blue.
I gaze upon the sun,
Watching it move time after time.
I now notice that I'm getting weak,
I can see the roots of myself are beginning to
Shrivel and die.
Now that it is autumn
I feel like I am ready to die.
But my children will carry on to their new life
While I lie myself, dead.
Thus my life has ended in a way of natural life.
But the way of life will circle my children,
Like my life circled around myself.

Craig Taylor (15)
Sybil Elgar School (NAS), Southall

Autumn Haiku

The leaf falls off the
Tree when it rains it will help
The leaf change colour.

Jobe Manikiza (15)
Sybil Elgar School (NAS), Southall

Love

I gave you my love for you to touch
It's not that good, it's not that much
Because I didn't want to be apart
You were forever going to be in my heart.

You hurt me now and hurt me then
I want to be with you again
So tell me that it's not true
All my feelings are hidden from you.

I cried for ages because you're not here
I'll walk for miles just to be near
By reading this poem I hope you'll see
That you truly mean the world to me.

I feel like my heart
Is being ripped out
I feel I have to scream and shout
Please be with me and I'll be so nice
Because being with you is like paradise.

Charlotte Allan (14)
The Business Academy, Bexley

World War II

The most unusual thing I ever saw?
Thousands of ships crossing the channel.
Early morning, shivering together
Rocking in our carriages.

Wasting away, too tired to fire our guns
Like a bullet in your chest.
Sharing bread and water.
Alarms going on in our ears.

Sometimes I don't know what I am doing.
Captain's telling you to polish your boots and gun.
Smell of death coming.
Boats getting ready to drop with soldiers in them to go and fight.

The journey was long, now off to shore.
Lined up in fours, trapped around a metal boat.
Soldiers throwing up over the boat.
Soldiers kissing their cross on their dog tags.

Doors going down, soldiers getting shot.
Crying for their mothers on other boats.
People on fire running to the sea.
German guns firing at innocent people.
You don't understand a word I'm saying, do you?

Joseph Ryan (13)
The Business Academy, Bexley

Remembering White Terror

The most unusual thing I ever felt?
Snow.
As I saw the white rain fall from the deep, everlasting sky
I tried to run from the white rain
But it was no use.
As I tried to run faster
The wind was pulling the white terror down
Faster and faster
Until I saw my whole life before my eyes.
Finally the white terror
Touching my soft, pure five-year-old hands.

Louis Hamilton (13)
The Business Academy, Bexley

Kindness

Kindness is an act of respect
Helping people through a tough time
Who's that little boy on his own over there?
I'll go and ask if he's alright.

All those disrespectful people
Bullying all those innocent children
Don't worry about that boy over there
We'll just sit here and ignore it.

Rebecca Brown (14)
The Business Academy, Bexley

Bending It

Have you ever tried to bend a bar
When you're so stressed out and you can't go far?

When you run upstairs rampaging to your room
Then shut the door behind you
And start to unblossom.

You cry and you sob and you sob and you cry
So many questions to ask, but who? But why?

At that precise moment you want everyone out
Of your room,
Of the life
You want no one to know about.

You hide all things from your mum and your dad
Don't cuddle me, I'm not a baby, not a lad.

When you're stressed out your day can't get any worse
You feel like hurting yourself, go beyond the nurse.

Your stressed out day has left you lonely and cold
You don't talk anymore
You don't feel neither big nor bold.

You get mad at your brothers, your sisters
At that precise moment
You feel like leaving them in blisters.

You get called for your dinner by your mum or your dad
But it's no surprise
It's a dinner you've already had.

Now your stressed out day has come to an end
There'll be peace tomorrow
There'll be nothing to bend.

Troy Ricketts (13)
The Business Academy, Bexley

All Her Love

She gives me all her love,
But only half the time.
But that half is all I need,
Baby.
Every time I'm on my own
I think of you

And him - he's not even there.
I love it when you kiss my neck.
I can just imagine

Others, they're just staring.
They all want what I've got.
But they're never, ever, ever,
Gonna get it

All the time, right?
Under my nose
I can still feel your lips.
Last time you were there,
I can still remember.
I can still hear

Him - he's not even there,
Why'd you bring it up?
Oh. No, not worried.

Sick. From missing the half of you
That I've got,
Baby.

Daniel Howell (16)
Therfield School, Leatherhead

Winter Sun Come Back

Winter sun, shining over
With its crisp white coat
And its dazzling clean strokes
I could watch and smell
And taste and touch it forever.

But sadly, the spring
With its bright light
Taking all traces of winter away
Giving warmth to the world
And everyone in it for now.

Winter sun will be
On its way once again
In seasons to come
It will be upon us
With radiant beauty once again.

Winter will be upon us soon
I will feel its place in me
Again.

Victoria Ludlow (14)
The Robert Napier School, Gillingham

An Egg

(Inspired by 'Valentine' by Carol Ann Duffy)

I give you an egg
If you're not careful it will break
It promises a broken heart
Which can never be fixed.

Sometimes it smells rotten
And the smell sticks with you
Forever.

I give you an egg
When boiled is greasy
Like hair.

I am only telling the truth
Not an emerald or a gem
But an egg.

Take it, I am giving you
What you are . . .
An egg.

Amber Cloughley (11)
The Robert Napier School, Gillingham

Falling

She felt as though she was as small as an ant.
She couldn't speak to anyone.
Her parents were like they spoke another language
And her friends were difficult.
No one could stop her when she was falling, falling.

She always felt at home near the sea
And she wished she were a fish.
She decided that when she died this is where she wanted to be.
No one could catch her when she was falling, falling.

Maybe she could die now
She could jump into the sea and drown.
So she did, she jumped.
No one could catch her or stop her when she was falling, falling.

Splash!

She had stopped falling, falling.
Her body would lie at the bottom of the sea forever.
There she was at home
And there she was happy.

Gemma Murrow (13)
The Robert Napier School, Gillingham

An Egg

(Inspired by 'Valentine' by Carol Ann Duffy)

I give you an egg
It has a hard shell
Protecting the good bits in the yolk
It promises minerals
Like a lover who cares.

An egg also creates life
A new start to our relationship
I give you an egg
When boiled the softness and tenderness
Reminds me of you.

I'm only telling the truth
Not a diamond ring or a gem
But an egg.

Take it
It means everything to me
And how much
I love you!

Amy Carr (11)
The Robert Napier School, Gillingham

The Winter Trees

The woods are filled with a soft dew
And the frost begins to shimmer
The forest leaves start anew
And the woodland light starts to dimmer

The robins come with their red breasts
And the swallows seek warm havens
The little children put on their vests
And the hedgehogs build their dirt dens

The sledges start to be used on hills
And the gloves and scarves are taken
The parents get their Christmas bills
And the stomachs are filled with bacon

The chickens get a massacre
The crackers are all being bought
A small child gets a chocolate bar
And presents are being sought

The woods are filled with a soft dew
And the frost begins to shimmer
The forest leaves start anew
And the woodland light starts to dimmer.

Benjamin Prince (13)
The Warriner School, Bloxham

In Remembrance Of

For R

I sing the song of an empty room,
Of the coldest night and the deepest gloom.

Where shadows of people,
With voices so cold,
Lament for the times,
That have now grown old.

Sadness is coming,
To pierce like a dart,
The cold, broken sphere,
That once was my heart.

I sing the song of the burning pain,
Of standing alone in the burning rain.

Waves crash around me,
Chilling my blood,
In my heart I am drowning,
The tide is in flood.

The barriers they fall,
Tumbling down in our eyes,
The people they call.
Await the fated hour.

I sing the song of the death I must die,
From life's first breath to final cry.

It's time
To say
Goodbye.

Helena Longman (14)
Townley Grammar School for Girls, Bexleyheath

My Secret

My secret follows me wherever I may go,
My secret makes me feel so depressed and low,
My secret eats way at me, although it doesn't show,
My secret is what's caused my life to be filled with sorrow.

If I told you my secret, the consequence would be,
A lifetime full of woe, with neither you nor me,
A lifetime full of hatred, where love should have been,
A lifetime with no happiness ever to be seen.

I wish I could tell you but it isn't easy,
I doubt that you will able to believe me,
So now I must go, to a place you can't see,
Please, it's no use trying to find me.

I'll say goodbye now, oh how it hurts,
Seeing you sleeping, while I'm at my worst,
I'll go now, quietly, so you won't awake,
Please, I beg you, don't cry for my sake.

I never deserved you, well, that was clear,
Even still, you stuck by me all these years,
But now my mistake is too big to forgive,
I can't bear to tell you, I'd rather not live.

I know I've probably hurt you more this way,
But at least my mistake won't be here to stay,
I've gone now, forget me, I'm not worth the pain,
Anguish, despair, I've hurt you again.

Jaskiran Sandhu (15)
Townley Grammar School for Girls, Bexleyheath

The Four Seasons Of The Year

Everything is covered in a blanket of white,
Nothing much can be seen in this sight.
The sun is hidden and gone away,
To only come back out in May.
It's gloomy, cold and wet,
This is how the winter weather is set!

The clouds are clearing away,
Tiptoeing far from today.
The new are now born,
The light shines on the flowers before dawn.
Let's dance and sing,
It's spring, it's spring!

It's a midsummer's day,
All the playful children say.
Strawberry, chocolate and vanilla, the flavours we love,
As pure and delightful as a dove.
Let's go to the fair,
Summer is now here!

Flowers have fallen to the floor,
In front of everyone's doors.
Red, orange, gold and brown,
Brings to faces mournful frowns.
Against the weather there's no need to fight,
Let's welcome the autumn days and nights!

Sukhjit Kaur Gidda (14)
Villiers High School, Southall

Winter Wish

Soft snow cascades through the white winter sky
Freely flowing with the wind by its side
Clouds concealed by a white window
Rapidly releasing fun from the skies

Children come outside in joy and bliss
Absolutely astonished to see their wish
Eager and elated they feel the snow
Magically melting their fingertips

Streets shielded by the ways of winter
Cars covered from top to bottom
Parents panic to get to work
Whereas woeful children watch and say goodbye

Sobbing slowly as their panicking parents bring them inside
Glum girls get ready for school while
Bad-tempered boys refuse to listen
Careless children carry on deceiving

Worryingly watching through the hazy windows
Patient parents watch the snow
Gradually going into the ground
Breathless boys and gasping girls
With ease watch their wish wilt away.

Karen Jay Dhande (14)
Villiers High School, Southall

Beggars

As I walked through the road
I saw two children sitting
Begging to the people around them
I saw incomplete dreams, wishes

In their tearful eyes
'I need food to eat,'
A child said who was bearing hunger
For the last three days

His friend looked at him
With his poor, helpless eyes
A passion of increment
Was agitating him completely

I quickly bought two sandwiches
And gave to those children
Surprise, happiness and pleasure
In their eyes, I suddenly felt

Satisfaction and proud of myself
Those two children were eating
Sandwiches as if they would
Never see the food again

I went back to my home
Thinking about our duties to other people
Are we satisfied with our lives
Or is something going wrong?

Ambreen Ahmed (14)
Villiers High School, Southall

Love

Love is everything,
Love is life,
Love is death.

Love is everything,
Love makes one do good,
Love makes one do bad.

Love is everything,
Love is living for,
Love is dying for.

Love is everything,
Love is to admire,
Love is to envy.

Love is everything,
Love is one,
Love is all.

Love is everything,
Love is life,
Love is death.

Deepraj Singh Sura (16)
Villiers High School, Southall

Witness Of Life

As deep as the ocean
They reveal all emotion
Whether happy and bright
Or as dark as the night
The window through which we read the heart
Each day they open at the start
To record each moment of life we pass
Read each emotion through the perfect, clear glass
And as we go on they get old and weak
Until they finally close, the tears will leak.

Sukhdeep Kaur Nagpal (14)
Villiers High School, Southall

School!

School is a precious gift in life.
It's a place to read.
A place to learn,
A place to write,
A place to learn!
I wonder what would happen
If teachers weren't born?
I guess our education
Would just be torn.
We are really lucky
To be in school
I've got to admit
School is kinda cool.
I'm really glad to be in Villiers High
And I will never let our school motto die!

Farah Choudhry (13)
Villiers High School, Southall

The Sea

My minions dancing round my feet,
Leaving their mark behind them.
Little elves in shapes of waves,
Running back and forth with never-ending will,
Casting their magic wherever they step.

The ocean full of magical creatures,
Enchanted coral with rainbow leaves,
Glistening in the ocean's sun.

Watching her move elegantly towards the horizon,
Her long blue hair following swiftly behind her,
Soon to be lost in a blurry haze,
Leaving her song to soothe us.

Jaskiran Kaur Chohan (15)
Villiers High School, Southall

Train

What is it? When did it get there?
She runs across the hills and valleys,
The wind blows her hair like clouds,
She's like a bullet from a gun,
She gets fed with mouth-watering coals.
I am the queen of the world, she races,
'Choooo, choooo,' that's what they say.
She's always on the go.

She's as long as a giraffe,
She enters dark, long mazes,
Blocking the bright light bulb sun.

Children, all ages, all sizes,
Women, men, all excited.
This is the time of their lives as they enter this ride of fame.
She leaves behind a trail like a snail,
She's always determined to go faster every day.

But when the moon is out to say goodnight,
She closes her eyes, as tomorrow is a new day.

Kisha Makepeace (13)
Villiers High School, Southall

Summer

Summer, summer, summer
Oh beautiful summer
How you shine your bright sun upon us
Gazing from the light blue sky
You make the flowers beam with colour
Red, orange, yellow and blue
Children screaming, laughing too
No jumpers, no coats, no thick socks
Instead us wearing thin, little frocks
Everyone enjoying ice cream at the park
Where I lay down with my family
Gazing at the sky bright blue
Playing with the sand on the beach
My family dig me in
Along comes the wave
Sprays itself at me
I soak myself like a dog would
I never want summer to end
But, oh well, it will come again
In the end.

Amandeep Marway (14)
Villiers High School, Southall

All Alone . . .

Without a care in the world,
I decided that I was going to walk alone.
I was going to be happy only this way,
That's how I hoped it would stay.

Every day passed within a blink of an eye,
All I was now good at was to cry.
Though I thought I was coping, it was tough,
Yet I always felt as if I'd had enough.

How I longed to be back at home,
Would everything by turned upside down? If only I had known.
If I could just take back every word I said,
Before I turned my back and fled.

Life is unfair but I have to face it.
I never thought staying alone would be the hardest bit.
I know I can't turn back time to the happy days,
But those memories are with me . . . always.

Reema Singh (14)
Villiers High School, Southall

Black And White

Black looks like a velvet blanket
Filled with dancing, shimmering stars.
White looks like the fluttering of angels' wings
Flapping faster than cars.
Black sounds like the haunting howl of the wind
As it tears through the trees at night.
White sounds like the serenity that embraces you
Like a tightly fitting glove which leaves you without a fright.
Black smells like the burnt charcoal
Which keeps you warm.
White smells like the stirring of hot milk
Which motions like a storm.
Black tastes like the dark, delicate, devouring chocolate
Which comforts you like a hug.
White tastes like a cappuccino's white, fluffy cloud
Covering the top of the mug.
Black feels like the peaceful touch of the dark angel.
White feels like the touch blessed by an angel.

Harmeet Sidhu (14)
Villiers High School, Southall

Autumn

As the season for autumn draws near
The crimson reds, sun-blushed yellows
And husk orange leaves fall to the ground
The moist, soil-enriched ground
With its bright, effervescent colours

The bare, lifeless trees sway in the cool, chilled air
As the squirrels scurry and bury their acorns
To hide them from their own
And to get ready for hibernation

As the twilight sun rises over the dew-dropped blades of grass
The dusk sky embraces the hues of yellows and pink
Of the out burn sun

There's no sign of the flowers which blossomed two months ago
But soon the flowers will once again grow
And sway in the cool, summer breeze.

Hasnat Chaudhry (14)
Villiers High School, Southall

Spring

The season of happiness and freedom,
Looking at the sky, going to the seaside.
Joy and laughter all around,
New lives being born.

Daffodils flourishing along with blossom,
All of the streets covered in a sheet of pink.
The light breeze blowing through your hair,
Why does the world seem so colourful?

The sun shines so bright,
Like a star that shines forever.
The leaves start to turn green,
And the birds sing sweetly.

Yes, it's that season,
It's spring!

Daljeet Kauldhar (14)
Villiers High School, Southall

Speak Now Or Forever Hold Your Peace

Everything looks so empty,
As I look around the room.
Why did you not stay with me?
Why did you have to go?

Is there something you need to tell me?
Then now's your perfect time,
There's only one thing that's killing me,
The silence here tonight.

Don't look over your shoulder,
And pray there's something there
To stop you from telling me
The truth that's always been there.

You never seem to understand
The torment you create.
Every time my eyes meet yours,
My heart is torn in two.

Everything looks so empty,
As I look around the room.
Just tell me quickly, tell me now,
Or never speak a word.

Indusha Selvanathar (15)
Wallington High School for Girls, Wallington

The End Of The World

(A poem in memory of the thousands of lives lost in the Asian tsunami)

It was once a beautiful evening,
With the waves lapping and licking . . .
At tiny feet, as children played.
The sun smiled its sweet blessing.

Suddenly, a tremendous wave came,
Thundering upon the fragile, delicate
Coast of God's paradise, on His Earth;
Serenity and tranquillity replaced by death.

The deadly water poured its toxic
Venom into generations of families,
Enveloping them in a cocoon of
Fear and pain.

The sea elevated to terrifying heights,
And plunged into the throats of
Innocent lives, too weak to
Hold on to their loved ones' hands.

And swept away, into the depths of the sea.
Forever and ever.
Never to return.

Indusha Selvanathar (15)
Wallington High School for Girls, Wallington

Cats

Cats can bounce,
Cats can pounce,
All cats purr,
And have soft fur,
Cats sleep all day,
And play all night,
Then jump out and give you a *fright!*

Rebecca Dear (11)
Walmer School, Walmer

Beyond Imagination

(Inspired by 'Dulce et Decorum est' by Wilfred Owen)

What bodies from wreckage, saved is a relief.
The dying, the screaming, the splattering of blood.
The ones who thought it was glorious.
Bodies scattered, scattered like seeds come to grow.
Rattling rifles seem no remorse
From fire, fire burning brighter than ever
Killing the ones for their country.
The scrunch and crunch of the bones
And the wagon which carried on.
Guttering, choking the sounds of drowning.
Six of which die behind.
Many of which come to follow the path.
The ecstasy of fumbling, as the gas oozes in.
Gas masks! 'Which we aren't a fried . . .'
It remains and coats the sky as far as the eye can see.
The dead, who rot, can't be gone near without a gas mask.
It's foul, worse than ever thought, worse than imaginable.
Lightning strikes of bullets which fade in distance.
The pyramids of us are too hard to bear.
My friend Henry was killed - shot through the head.
I nearly suffered from shell-shock and many more suffered worse.
I tell you, dear lady, the one near the fire,
The one at home that is,
War isn't the honourable thing of saving our country or doing well
And the idealist thoughts which follow.
War is the spraying, suffering and guttering of bullets
Then drowning.
We have no choice; we'll get shot by our own men if we retreat.
Killed by the ones we thought not of in bad name.
Many have gone syphilitic, blind, lame or died in the sludge.
Seeing them die feels more bitter than the cud.
I leave you now, with us fighting with innocent, desperate glory
And *Dulce et decorum est.*
Pro patria mori.

Elliot Langley-Smith (13)
Whitton Secondary School, Whitton

White And Green

The mud squelches under my boots
The rain is fast devouring our muddied ditch
I stand next to my fellow colleagues, friends, family
The sergeant is barking orders
Over the thunderous sounds of the rain
Oh how I long to see white and green
We peer over the ditch into the vast battlefield
Littered with mutilated bodies
The remaining 7 seconds of our lives fast approach
It seems that the world around us has come to a pause
Oh how I long to see white and green
We hear the cries of the Hun
We leap onto the battlefield
Screaming, our voices hoarse
All I see is red and brown
Oh how I long to see white and green
We fight, fight for our lives
Alas, no more red or brown
I see white and green . . .

Nabeel Vohra (14)
Whitton Secondary School, Whitton

Florida Fun

We went abroad to see the sun,
We went to Florida.
We flew from Gatwick quite nearby,
And then we hired a car.

We had a villa with a pool,
Not far from Orlando.
We went to theme parks every day,
Until my mum said, 'No.'

'There's more to life than fun,' she said,
'We must improve our brains.
We'll go to Cape Canaveral,
Unless, of course, it rains.'

It didn't rain I'm glad to say,
Because we saw the place
Where the rockets stand upright
Before they fly to space.

Vicky Alcock (12)
Whitton Secondary School, Whitton